I0130362

SOCIAL MEDIA IMAGES AND CONFLICTS

This collection considers how digital images and social media reconfigure the way conflicts are played out, represented and perceived around the globe.

Devoted to developing original theoretical frameworks and empirical insights, the volume addresses the role of user images and social media in relation to urgent subjects such as public opinion and emotion, solidarity, evidence and verification, censorship and fake news, which are all central to the ways current conflicts are represented and unfold. Essays include a unique range of case studies from different regional and political contexts (Middle East, Europe, Asia, North America) and in connection with different conflict types (war, terror, riots, everyday resistance, etc.). They also consider performative genres such as memes, selfies and appropriations as well as images conforming to the realism and authenticity of conventional photojournalism. In this way, the collection responds to the challenges of swiftly evolving image genres as well as to the continually shifting policies and algorithms of commercial digital platforms.

Together, the essays offer innovative theories and exemplary case studies as a resource for teaching and research in media, journalism and communication programmes. It is also relevant to students, teachers and researchers within sociology, political science, anthropology and related fields.

Mette Mortensen is Professor and Deputy Head of Department at the Department of Communication, University of Copenhagen, Denmark. She specializes in visual media studies and was Principal Investigator of the collective research projects "Images of Conflict, Conflicting Images" (2017–2022) funded by the Velux Foundation. She is the author or editor of eight books, including the monograph *Eyewitness Images and Journalism: Digital Media, Participation, and Conflict* (Routledge 2015) and, most recently, the volume *Social Media Materialities and Protest: Critical Reflections* co-edited with Christina Neumayer and Thomas Poell (Routledge 2019).

Ally McCrow-Young is a postdoctoral researcher at the Department of Communication, Section of Media Studies at the University of Copenhagen, Denmark. Her research focuses on emerging, and primarily visual, technologies and digital culture. Ally is a core member of the research group "Images of Conflict, Conflicting Images" which explores how digital images and connective media transform the way conflicts are represented. Her doctoral work "Incongruent Images: Connective Mourning Rituals on Instagram Following the 2017 Manchester Arena Attack" (2020) examined the intersection of violent conflicts, visual social media and everyday images.

SOCIAL MEDIA IMAGES AND CONFLICTS

*Edited by Mette Mortensen and
Ally McCrow-Young*

Routledge
Taylor & Francis Group

LONDON AND NEW YORK

First published 2023
by Routledge
4 Park Square, Milton Park, Abingdon, Oxon OX14 4RN

and by Routledge
605 Third Avenue, New York, NY 10158

Routledge is an imprint of the Taylor & Francis Group, an informa business

© 2023 selection and editorial matter, Mette Mortensen and Ally McCrow-Young; individual chapters, the contributors

The right of Mette Mortensen and Ally McCrow-Young to be identified as the authors of the editorial material, and of the authors for their individual chapters, has been asserted in accordance with sections 77 and 78 of the Copyright, Designs and Patents Act 1988.

All rights reserved. No part of this book may be reprinted or reproduced or utilised in any form or by any electronic, mechanical, or other means, now known or hereafter invented, including photocopying and recording, or in any information storage or retrieval system, without permission in writing from the publishers.

Trademark notice: Product or corporate names may be trademarks or registered trademarks, and are used only for identification and explanation without intent to infringe.

British Library Cataloguing-in-Publication Data
A catalogue record for this book is available from the British Library

Library of Congress Cataloging-in-Publication Data
Names: Mortensen, Mette, 1971– editor. | McCrow-Young, Ally, editor.
Title: Social media images and conflicts / edited by Mette Mortensen
and Ally McCrow-Young.
Description: Abingdon, Oxon; New York, NY: Routledge, 2023. |
Includes bibliographical references and index.
Identifiers: LCCN 2022020803 (print) | LCCN 2022020804 (ebook) |
ISBN 9781032010557 (hbk) | ISBN 9781032010564 (pbk) |
ISBN 9781003176923 (ebk)
Subjects: LCSH: Social media–Research. | Digital images–Social aspects. |
Conflict of interests. | Emotions–Social aspects.
Classification: LCC HM742 .S62819633 2023 (print) |
LCC HM742 (ebook) | DDC 302.23/1–dc23/eng/20220518
LC record available at https://lccn.loc.gov/2022020803
LC ebook record available at https://lccn.loc.gov/2022020804

ISBN: 978-1-032-01055-7 (hbk)
ISBN: 978-1-032-01056-4 (pbk)
ISBN: 978-1-003-17692-3 (ebk)

DOI: 10.4324/9781003176923

Typeset in Bembo
by Newgen Publishing UK

CONTENTS

TABLES

CONTRIBUTORS

Stuart Allan is Professor in the School of Journalism, Media and Culture at Cardiff University, UK. Much of his research revolves around the visual dimensions of war, conflict and crisis reporting, including both professional and citizen photojournalism. He is currently preparing a history of war photography, titled *Conflicting Images*, for Routledge. Recent publications include *Journalism, Gender and Power* (Routledge, 2019), co-edited with Cynthia Carter and Linda Steiner.

Bolette B. Blaagaard is an associate professor of Communication at Aalborg University, Copenhagen. She has worked extensively on the topic of citizen journalism and citizen media, including the publications *Citizen Journalism as Conceptual Practice* (Rowman & Littlefield, 2018), *Citizen Media and Public Spaces* (Routledge, 2016) co-edited with Mona Baker and the *Routledge Encyclopedia of Citizen Media* (Routledge, 2020) co-edited with Mona Baker, Henry Jones, Luis Pérez-González. She is also the co-editor of the Routledge book series *Critical Perspectives on Citizen Media*.

Jun Liu is an associate professor in the Department of Communication at the University of Copenhagen, Denmark and Research affiliate, Center on Digital Culture and Society, The Annenberg School for Communication, University of Pennsylvania. He publishes in the fields of sociology, political science, communication and computer science in journals such as *New Media & Society, Journal of the Association for Information Science and Technology* and *European Journal of Sociology*. He has won awards from the American Political Science Association and the International Communication Association. His latest publication is *Shifting Dynamics of Contention in the Digital Age* (Oxford University Press, 2020).

Ally McCrow-Young is a postdoctoral researcher at the Department of Communication, Section of Media Studies at the University of Copenhagen, Denmark. Her research focuses on emerging, and primarily visual, technologies and digital culture. Ally is a core member of the research group "Images of Conflict, Conflicting Images" which explores how digital images and connective media transform the way conflicts are represented. Her doctoral work *Incongruent Images: Connective Mourning Rituals on Instagram Following the 2017 Manchester Arena Attack* (2020) examined the intersection of violent conflicts, visual social media and everyday images.

Saumava Mitra is an assistant professor at the School of Communications of Dublin City University in Ireland. His research focuses on identifying the gendered and geopolitical inequities inherent in photographs of – and acts surrounding photographing – violent and social conflicts. He is interested in both the questions of how these inequities are inscribed into the photographic images of conflicts as well as the effects of these inequities on the lives and livelihoods of those who produce these images. Prior to joining DCU, Mitra worked in journalism, communications and in academia in South Asia, East Africa, North and Central Americas and Western Europe.

Mette Mortensen is Professor and Deputy Head of Department at the Department of Communication, University of Copenhagen. She specializes in visual media studies and is the Principal Investigator of the collective research projects "Images of Conflict, Conflicting Images" (2017–2022) funded by the Velux foundation. She is the author or editor of eight books, including the monograph *Eyewitness Images and Journalism. Digital Media, Participation, and Conflict* (Routledge 2015) and, most recently, the volume *Social Media Materialities and Protest: Critical Reflections* co-edited with Christina Neumayer and Thomas Poell (Routledge 2019).

Christina Neumayer is an associate professor of Media Studies at the Department of Communication at the University of Copenhagen. Her research focuses on the role of digital media technologies, platforms and data for political contention, protest, activism, racism, civic engagement, social movements and, more broadly, political communication. Her most recent publications include the volume *Social Media Materialities and Protest: Critical Reflections* (Routledge, 2019) co-edited with Mette Mortensen and Thomas Poell.

Sandra Ristovska is an assistant professor in Media Studies at the College of Media, Communication and Information at the University of Colorado Boulder. She studies how images shape the pursuit of human rights and social justice with a particular focus on institutional and legal decision-making contexts. She is the author of *Seeing Human Rights: Video Activism as a Proxy Profession* (MIT Press, in press) and co-editor of *Visual Imagery and Human Rights Practice* (Palgrave, 2018). Ristovska is an affiliated fellow with the Information Society Project at Yale Law and the Center for Media, Data and Society at Central European University.

Luca Rossi is associate professor of Digital Media and Networks at the Department of Digital Design of IT University of Copenhagen. He is member of the "Networks Data and Society" (NERDS) and coordinates the "Human Centred Data Science" research group. His interdisciplinary research tries to connect tradiGonal socio-logical theory with computaGonal approaches. Within this line of research, he has worked and published in the context of online parGcipaGon, online acGvism, poliGcal campaign and elecGon studies.

Brenda Witherspoon is an associate teaching professor in the Greenlee School of Journalism and Communication at Iowa State University in Ames, Iowa. She previ-ously worked as a professional journalist, and her current research collaborations focus on photojournalism in the Global South. Recent publications include "Invisible in This Visual World? Work and Working Conditions of Female Photographers in the Global South", *Journalism Studies*, 2022, co-written with Saumava Mitra and Sara Creta.

ACKNOWLEDGEMENTS

We are most grateful to the many colleagues, collaborators and friends who have supported and inspired us in developing this volume. First and foremost, we are very thankful to the authors of this volume; it has indeed been a pleasure to work with you.

This volume grows out of the work from the research project *Images of Conflict, Conflicting Images*, funded by the Velux Foundation's Core Group Grant (2017–2022), at the Department of Communication, University of Copenhagen. We would like to express our gratitude to the Velux Foundation for supporting the research conducted for this volume and our previous work. We are immensely grateful to all of the core group members of *Images of Conflict, Conflicting Images* – Bolette B. Blaagaard, Solveig Gade, Jun Liu, Nina Grønlykke Mollerup, Christina Neumayer and Ekatherina Zhukova. It has been a privilege and pleasure collaborating with all of you, and we are most thankful for the supportive and constructive research environment.

We would also like to thank Anne Gjelsvik, Aurora Hoel, Ingvild Folkvord, Nadége Lourme and Mads Outzen, who are members of the research group *Face of Terror: Understanding Terrorism from the Perspective of Critical Media Aesthetics* (Norwegian Research Council 2016–2020) based at the Norwegian University of Science and Technology in Trondheim. We greatly value our research collaborations and have learnt so much from discussing our shared interests in conflicts and visual media with you.

We are grateful to colleagues and friends for enriching collaborations that have informed this volume in direct and indirect ways: Stuart Allan, Tina Askanius, Lilie Chouliaraki, Lina Dencik, Mikkel Fugl Eskjær, Lene Hansen, Annette Hill, Maja Horst, Stig Hjarvard, Andrew Hoskins, Anne Jerslev, Nete Nørgaard Kristensen,

Marwan M. Kraidy, Mervi Pantti, Thomas Poell, Chris Peters, Lisa Richey, Anastasia K. Røren, Hans-Jörg Trenz and Louise Wolthers.

Thanks also to Nina Jerslev Svendsen for competent research assistance. Last, but not least, we would like to thank Natalie Forster and Tanushree Baijal at Routledge.

INTRODUCTION

Social Media Images and Conflicts: Power, Proximity and Performativity

Mette Mortensen and Ally McCrow-Young

As we finalise this book in March 2022, Russia has invaded Ukraine, sparking the largest European conflict between sovereign states since World War II. In these first few days of the conflict, we are seeing images of casualties on both sides, of Ukrainians taking shelter in underground metro stations and parking lots, of Russian ground forces and tanks moving towards Kyiv, of mileage long lines of cars as Ukrainian citizens prepare to flee, of damage and destruction. Social media users across the world are creating tribute posts and re-sharing support resources. Meanwhile, Ukrainian President Volodymyr Zelenskyy releases selfie videos from the streets of Kyiv, addressing fellow Ukrainians and the outside world. Streams of propaganda also circulate online, such as satirical Russian-backed films belittling Ukrainians or fabricating evidence of Ukrainian aggression by repurposing social media footage and other content as pretext for the invasion (Borger et al. 2022; Harding 2022). Sifting through these various visual testimonies, satellite documentation, citizen commentary, propaganda and tribute posts paints an overwhelming and complex picture of the conflict. As the war itself and the news reporting continue to develop, so too do these streams of images evolve across media.

The invasion of Ukraine is the most recent example of the changing role of images in conflicts. Throughout the 20th century, images from conflicts were controlled, curated and censored in interplays between mass media, state and military. Digital cameras and later smartphones have enabled people to record their first-hand impressions of conflicts. Images are produced and spread in abundance by citizens, activists, soldiers, trolls, terrorists, whistle-blowers and more in today's media, distinguished by platform convergence and blurred boundaries between media production and consumption. As a result, news media no longer enjoy monopoly on conflict reporting and state/military are no longer able to fully manage the image flow.

DOI: 10.4324/9781003176923-1

Understanding the shifting role of images in conflicts is of pressing scholarly and societal importance. Digital media not only change how conflicts are represented. Conflicts themselves change as the more uncontrollable image flow contributes to shape, escalate and de-escalate conflicts – or even to create new conflicts. This volume concerns how digital images and social media reconfigure the way conflicts are played out, represented and perceived. Images are mobilised as sites of resistance and protest, called upon and debated as evidence, shared as commemorative acts following violent attacks, regulated and censored, accused of being misinformative, appropriated and repurposed, and (dis)ordered in increasingly complex systems. Chapters in this volume address the myriad and often-diverging character of images on social media that emerge through, and in response to, conflict: Who are the actors taking, mobilising and verifying images? How are these images understood and how do they come to represent conflicts? What vested interests are involved in promoting or disputing their significance and legitimacy, and in which ways do they impact online and offline worlds? Furthermore, what role is played by social media platforms in determining which images we see or do not see from conflicts?

Actors, Images, Platforms

The history of social media images and conflicts spans less than two decades. Social media were initially lauded for their democratic potential to empower citizens and increase public access to diverse images from conflicts, expressed in hopeful idioms such as a YouTube revolution and Twitter revolution, coined in relation to, for example, the Iranian post-Election protests (2009) and the revolutions in Tunisia (2010–2011) and Egypt (2011) (e.g. Castells 2012; Jenkins et al. 2016; Shirky 2008). Along these lines, scholars pointed to the participatory potential of social media, their ease of use, speed of interaction and ability to host otherwise marginalised viewpoints and experiences (e.g. Khamis and Vaughn 2012; Mottahedeh 2015). Sceptics later warned against fake news, disinformation, misinformation and information overload, as well as the casual spread of footage that is violent, confidential or may compromise safety and security (e.g. Jones 2021; Rogers and Niederer 2020). Most recently, there has been increasing awareness of how the commercial imperatives of platforms and the regulatory policies such as censorship practices shape narratives and discourses on conflicts in ways that are difficult to see through for media users (e.g. Liu and Zhao 2021; Madenga, 2021; Ngoshi 2021; Nowak 2021).

This volume centres on the paradoxes pertaining to social media images and conflicts. Social media greatly enhance visibility and agency for actors on the ground in conflicts, while the very same social media contexts simultaneously raise questions of veracity, proportionality and economic incentives. They amplify opportunities for creative, political and social participation with conflict events, however, they also influence the kinds of images that are produced and shared by users. Such images are often constrained by algorithmic favouring of the dramatic and spectacular, by the fleeting formation of "affective publics" (Papachirissi 2015) and by genre conventions determining which aspects of conflicts are shown and how.

The eight chapters in this volume focus on the relationship between images, participatory platforms and global conflicts. The volume offers a range of case studies of digital images produced and disseminated by participants from different regional/political contexts (Middle East, Europe, Asia, North America) and in relation to different conflict types (war, terror, riots, everyday resistance, civil rights). Within these regions and cases, the chapters also address a diversity of platform contexts, such as Facebook, Weibo, Instagram, YouTube and Twitter, examining the interplay between specific platform dynamics and the images that they host.

To analyse the proliferation of social media images from conflicts, the chapters employ both qualitative and quantitative methods derived from social sciences, humanities and digital humanities. The range of methodological approaches adopted throughout the volume offers different analytical entry points in response to the challenges of image abundance and continually shifting policies and algorithms of commercial digital platforms. In this way, the volume contributes to discussions about how research might better understand rich, contextual and lavish visual data from various global conflicts, spanning from depictions of violence to expressions of the everyday in areas of combat.

This book is structured according to three perspectives: actors, images and platforms. The first three chapters explore issues related to the *actors* involved in producing, publishing, mobilising and vetting images. These chapters focus on the precarious labour performed by individuals documenting conflicts in their immediate area and the evolving roles of (citizen) photojournalists, human rights collectives and news media. The next two chapters focus on *images*, addressing the way visuals circulated on social media operate within a continuum between realism and performativity, and what this means for their political mobilisation. The final three chapters delve into *platforms*, the site of dissemination and the ways in which policies, structures and top-down regulation impact image practices and prominence. In the following, we present and contextualise the book according to these three perspectives.

Proximity and Precarity in Taking, Sharing and Assessing Images

Social media images from conflicts reflect and are the result of emerging and evolving forms of labour. They are distinguished by *proximity* as individuals report on conflicts in their local regions, as well as *precarity* in terms of physical safety, work status and economic livelihood.

The nearness to events characterising much visual conflict reporting tips the balance traditionally maintained within photojournalism between proximity and distance. To understand this, we need to take a step back and consider how proximity, an enduring ideal for visual reporting to secure authentic, immediate and realistic images from conflict areas, has traditionally been counterbalanced by distance in both a normative and geographic sense. It constitutes another journalistic ideal to keep critical distance to ensure objective and fair reporting (see, e.g. Allan and Zelizer 2004). Moreover, visual conflict reporting has mostly been aimed at faraway audiences; news media in the Global North have traditionally held near-monopoly over visual conflict reporting on distant others, predominantly from the Global South, with the intention of evoking interest in, and compassion for, their suffering (e.g. Boltanski 1999; Chouliaraki 2006). Conflict reporters have managed this balance between proximity and distance within the institutional confines of news media, news agencies, etc.

Social media have reconfigured visual conflict reporting. Images taken by people transmitting their situated and embodied experience of conflicts typically do not project distance in a normative sense, that is, they usually show conflicts from an immediate, first-hand, decontextualised and subjective point of view. When conflicts are documented by people who are themselves part of it, core journalistic values of objectivity, authority and autonomy become unsettled (e.g. Andén-Papadopoulos and Pantti 2011; 2013; Allan 2013; Mortensen 2015). This leaves us with the key question of how we are to assess and understand the knowledge, experience and emotion conveyed in these visual testimonies (see also Chouliaraki and Mortensen 2022). As Karin Wahl-Jorgensen maintains, these visuals are often seen as the "uncensored outpouring of personal storytelling, emotional integrity, realism, immediacy and identification" in contrast to the perceived professional distance of journalism, which involves a "… "cold," "detached," "objective" and "distanced" approach" (Wahl-Jorgensen 2015, 172). Much is left up to the viewer, and this has generated a new infrastructure for contextualising, fact-checking and verifying images, undertaken by photographers themselves as well as human rights collectives, mainstream news media, news agencies and more.

The proximity in reporting conflict through social media comes with the cost of precarity. Individuals taking up the ad hoc labour of documenting local conflicts often have to work under conditions of physical, professional and economical precarity in what Yazbeck (2021) describes as "… a complex, hierarchical ecology of newsmaking that marginalises those it depends on for coverage". In the case of armed conflicts such as the civil war in Syria, international news media depended to a high degree on images by local media workers operating on social media because it has been deemed too dangerous for their own correspondents to report from combat zones (see also Mollerup and Mortensen 2020). This has pushed the boundaries traditionally upheld between professional and non-professional photographers, whether the latter are referred to as amateurs, witnesses, citizen journalists, citizens, activists, etc. These competing designations point to the unclear role of these actors, and the equally unclear status of their work.

The combination of these two factors – proximity and precarity – characterises the work and working conditions of individuals and collectives taking and mobilising, as well as vetting and contextualising images. The first three chapters in the volume address this development from the perspective of photographers, human rights collectives and the interplay between actors on the ground, social media, news media and NGOs.

Opening the volume, the chapter by Saumava Mitra and Brenda Witherspoon studies the impact of social media on the labour undertaken by what the authors refer to as the "most marginalised" and "least-studied group" of photographers: female photojournalists reporting from their local areas, regimes outside the West that are politically repressive, gender oppressive and ridden by conflicts. Mitra and Witherspoon point to the regularity with which freelance and temporary photojournalistic workers are replacing long-term employment, as well as the unauthorised use of these actors' images without compensation. Within this environment of precarious labour, social media are key for these photographers in their professionalisation process, in terms of facilitating self-promotion and seeking validation from peers and established media workers.

The study by Mitra and Witherspoon focuses on how these photojournalists traverse the lines between the personal and the professional, responding to the "gig economy" of social media, in which "relational labour" is key to "build social relationships that foster paid work" (Baym 2015, 16). Relational labour serves as an attempt to curtail their precarious working conditions (see also, e.g. Mollerup and Mortensen 2020; Yazbeck 2021). Moreover, these photographers also turn to relational labour to overcome the gendered, racialised and geocultural exclusions that they otherwise encounter. And finally, in gaining visibility through relational labour, they seek to remedy what they see as the misrepresentation of non-Western societies and disrespect for non-Western people in news images that typically overemphasise conflict and despair. They want instead to direct attention to scenes from everyday life to incite more specific and grounded forms of empathy and identification.

The chapter by Sandra Ristovska addresses how human rights collectives seek to solve verification challenges created by videos circulating on social media that document possible transgressions of human rights but are difficult to handle as sources due to their uncertain provenance and content. Produced for various purposes and by different actors (e.g. refugees, NGOs, whistleblowers, activists, military, law enforcement, terrorists), these videos nonetheless carry "evidentiary promise" to use a phrase from Alan Sekula (1986, 6). Human rights advocates have sought to professionalise video activism and they have also, Ristovska argues, developed "proxy professions", which claim authority as visual experts to render videos "meaningful as evidence". In charting the evolution of human rights video activism as a proxy profession, Ristovska sheds light on the central role of these visual experts, and the use of video as institutional evidence in supporting human rights. While the emergence of the proxy professional status aids human rights collectives in promoting evidentiary standards and policies for eyewitness video, this work is also constrained by institutional logics which evaluate and interrogate the proof value of visuals emerging from conflicts. The flow of conflict visuals that first emerge on social media before reaching mainstream news media is also part of this intricate negotiation between verification, curation and editorial protocols.

While the first two chapters study the developing role of photographers and human rights collectives in the visual news circuit, the chapter by Stuart Allan takes stock of the growing reliance on citizen-led photojournalistic labour by international news media, and what he terms the "use-value" of such images and labour.

Media outlets are increasingly involved in the collaborative process of verifying the authenticity of visuals during the editorial process. Allan examines the course of Syria's Civil War from 2011 onwards, which, as he writes, has been designated the "most collectively mediated conflict in history", as images have been weaponised and news media have depended to an unprecedented degree on "burgeoning participatory cultures".

Creating an overview of initiatives taken by citizens and activists documenting the civil war from an embodied and proximate point of view, Allan problematises the common-held, normative belief that photojournalism from conflict areas should be dispassionate and objective, let alone separate facts from values and emotions. Rather, he makes the plea that a "collective ethos of commitment" has manifested itself by the many photographers, professional and non-professional alike, putting their lives at risk to bear witness to pain and suffering, making claims to human rights and holding those in power responsible. In this way, Allan stresses the need to develop new approaches to the multitude of images emerging through social media from current conflicts.

These chapters together pose questions such as how are we to assess and understand social media images when we can no longer apply traditional normative beliefs pertaining to photojournalism? And where does it lead if we remove the standard editorial toolbox of source criticism and vetting that often seems to be inadequate? These questions become all the more pressing as we now turn our attention to the social media images themselves and how they blur boundaries between realism and performativity.

Mobilising Social Media Images: In between Realism and Performativity

This volume studies a wide range of images, from photographs taken by professional photojournalists to eyewitness images snapped by bystanders, to memes and other remixed images, to icons, to works created by artists or human rights' collectives. These varied images are united in that they are shared on social media and that they document or comment on conflictual events. But how do we systematise and make sense of these many different forms and genres of images? We propose that social media images from conflicts are to be understood within a continuum between realism and performativity.

Images circulated on social media from conflict zones are often associated with the realism of eyewitness footage taken by bystanders or participants who are first on the scene and provide an exclusive insight into unfolding events. These images have for over a decade consolidated themselves as a standard feature of conflict reporting; they are circulated en masse on social media and routinely featured in coverage by mainstream news media (e.g. Andén-Papadopoulos and Pantti 2011; Allan 2013; Mortensen 2015). The prominence of eyewitness images is explicable by the ease of production and dissemination as well as their recognisability; they adhere to key genre conventions of photojournalism such as realism, proximity and authenticity. At the same time, another tendency has manifested itself for user images from conflicts to be non-mimetic and performative. Genres such as memes, selfies, appropriations and cartoons have proliferated on social media and beyond over the past few years (e.g. Boudana, Frosh and Cohen 2017; McCrow-Young 2020; Mortensen 2017; Mortensen and Neumayer 2021; Olesen 2018). They use personal perspectives along with poetic modes, humour and satire to share information, opinions, experiences, beliefs, etc., and draw on online participatory cultures as well as the tradition within visual art for processing and expressing experiences of war.

While both realistic and performative images from conflicts have attracted solid scholarly attention, they are mostly treated as separate tendencies. This volume does not view a contradiction between realism and performativity but rather, as mentioned, sees them within a continuum of visual communication emerging from current conflicts. There are several reasons for this: the most conspicuous one is that genres merge and images are remixed, repurposed and recontextualised. For example, documentary photographs or eyewitness images often spawn memes and other appropriations in such a way that the "original" image is further spread and its authenticity used as point of departure for making a critical and/or humorous commentary on the depicted situation (e.g. Boudana, Frosh and Cohen 2017; Mortensen 2017; Zhukova 2022). Performative modes of expression, such as street art, may, on the other hand, be documented in "realistic" images (Blaagaard and Mollerup 2021), once again unsettling the idea of a binary between realism and performativity. Moreover, staged or performative modes may convey authentic experiences of the complexities of being in a conflict zone and in this way communicate about the "reality" of war. Indeed, as Solveig Gade contends, rather than being preoccupied with whether images are manipulated or not (because they are "most probably" in "one way or another"), we should instead think about how and why certain images are "imbued with truth-value" in grey zones between the evidentiary and the fictitious (Gade 2018, 42).

In addition to merging genres and formats, social media images – and especially the ones that attract attention and are politically mobilised – are characterised by their virality, which constitutes a performative aspect in itself. The photographic image has always been prone to enter into new contexts, and take on new meanings detached from the original circumstances, as has been firmly established in post-structuralist photo theory (e.g. Sekula 1986; Tagg 1988). Networked images take this to an extreme. Even if they have been "created with a specific purpose in mind", their reception often leads to "unforeseen and unintended effects", which are sometimes fatal (Eder and Klonk 2017, 3). This points to the performativity of media beyond representation (Cottle 2008, 138), and the sociability involved in social media images not only seeking to spread information and share experience, but also to establish and maintain networks and relationships through phatic communication and "connected presence" (Licoppe and Smoreda 2005). Donatella della Ratta even argues that "networked images" are performative to the extent that they have ceased to be grounded in social reality:

Networked images no longer aim at mirroring reality or conveying an ethical address. They have been transformed into an aesthetic performance intended to be reproduced, liked, and shared in the circuits of the social web. Their capacity to be injected into the networks' dynamics of "spreadability" generates their viral potential, which in turn forms a social currency that counts much more than any truth-value in the web's economy of attention and circulation.

No longer is visual media valued for its representations and mimic potential, for calling into being an "ethical regime" of the visual, for its quality of serving as "image evidence", or for its commitment to an adherence to reality.

Ratta 2021, 71–72, see also chapter by Stuart Allan, this volume

We agree with Ratta insofar as social media images engage in an "aesthetic performance". However, a red thread running through this volume is that the performativity of images does not rule out their commitment to documenting reality, providing evidence or summoning an "ethical regime", as Ratta puts it. But the co-existence of realism and performativity is uneasy. Performativity raises suspicion about the veracity of the images and feeds into discourses of fake news, misinformation, disinformation and propaganda. These discourses are habitually called upon to destabilise the information and knowledge transmitted through images and delegitimise their political claims – whether this mistrust is based on genuine doubts about authenticity or serves as an oft-visited argument against images that are politically threatening, risky or inconvenient.

The chapters by Mette Mortensen and Bolette B. Blaagaard address the potentials for political mobilisation emerging from the continuum of realism and performativity. Mortensen's conceptualisation of "social media icons" as images that first gain prominence on social media highlights the added scrutiny that these images face as a result of their original (and viral) connective context. She argues that social media icons are commonly received within a framework of evidence and emotion; these images are at once historically fixed to concrete events and carry an emotional plea as they come to symbolise more abstract notions of sacrifice, suffering and victimhood. Studying two different examples of social media icons from the Syrian Civil War, the "instant news icon" Omran Daqneesh (2016) and the "iconic actor" Bana Alabed (2016–), the chapter shows how evidence and emotion both condition and counteract one another. On the one hand, mobilisation through emotion is crucial for the virality of iconic images and for creating awareness of the specific incidents and broader issues of injustice and suffering that they procure evidence of. On the other hand, the collective emotional outcry renders social media icons vulnerable to allegations that they are manipulative, fake or propagandistic, designed to elicit emotion and to go viral. In the cases studied, this criticism constituted a way for the Syrian regime to repudiate the suffering of civilians documented by citing the performativity of social media icons to deflate their realism.

The chapter by Blaagaard likewise studies the space in between realism and performativity through which icons gain their meaning and are mobilised politically. In the context of the continued struggle for civil rights in the US, in which the Black Lives Matter movement has played a prominent part, the chapter analyses two artefacts of engagement and embodied gestures that accompanied the killings of Michael Brown (2014) with "Hands up, don't shoot" and Ahmaud Arbery (2020) with "#IRunWithMaud". Examining the entanglement of these embodied gestures and protest icons, Blaagaard interrogates implications of this confluence to the political discourses it produces. She argues that the images in these two cases go beyond clear-cut realism with documentation of violence, performing and producing counter-publics through gestures and visual expressions. The networked performativity involved in re-enacting the last words and final gestures of the murder victims on social media produces what Blaagaard alludes to as "double hashtags" that "generate critical memory and a black public sphere" which is enabled through "a black gaze", as she writes with reference to hooks (2015). Far from being monolithic, the double hashtags spawn political acts that produce two political discourses – through digital and material manifestations – one of vulnerability and one of endurance.

Both chapters in this section point to how the documentation on the spot of violent and deadly events, bounded as they are in the realism of eyewitness footage at the core of the studied cases, nonetheless is interpreted and appropriated in various performative ways to take advantage of the potential for political mobilisation in the depiction of innocent, civilian victims. The continuum between realism and performativity in these instances opens the door to acknowledging that the lives injured or lost matter, and to making political claims about justice and humanity. At the same time, the mobilising force in the continuum between realism and performative renders the imagery vulnerable to scepticism and criticism. Running beneath the patterns of political mobilisation discussed by Mortensen and Blaagaard is the commercial and regulatory infrastructure of social media, which is the subject of the third and final section of the volume.

Infrastructural Dynamics: Platforms, Policies and Regulation

The online dissemination of images from contemporary conflicts is shaped by bottom-up user engagement, top-down regulation and shifting platform policies. Such social media dynamics have been conceptualised with partially overlapping terms such as "social media logic" (van Dijck and Poell 2013), "affordances" (Hutchby 2001) and "networked media logics" (Klinger and Svensson 2014). These designations of online – and particularly social – media environments underscore the interaction between the technologies, economies and behaviours that inform contemporary social media dynamics.

Similarly, the relationship between platform-specific structures and user engagement has been highlighted in concepts such as "vernacular creativity" (Burgess 2006), referring to participatory user creativity involved in everyday cultural participation online, as well as "platform vernacular", designating the "shared (but not static) conventions and grammars of communication, which emerge from the ongoing interactions between platforms and users …" (Gibbs et al. 2014, 257). These conceptualisations emphasise the way platform-specific infrastructures, policies and user cultures facilitate, if not determine, the way meanings, opinions and emotions are co-produced around conflictual events. Such infrastructural codes and conventions mean that collective responses following conflict (and especially violent) events often assume new forms, intersecting with different publics as well as different – and often very tangential – themes and conversations. For instance, as social media are highly personalised, fluid spaces, issues such as grief and mourning following conflict events become part of a stream of irreverent content (Leaver and Highfield 2018, 31) rather than static places for remembrance (see also McCrow-Young 2020). The three final chapters in this volume examine this confluence of commercial, institutional and vernacular platform cultures, shedding light on how users share images, and how conflict events themselves are constituted through this interplay of infrastructural dynamics.

Social media platforms enable a plethora of alternative images and perspectives from a variety of actors in conflicts. However, the fluctuating policy and algorithmic landscape of these platforms often shift the power away from grassroots users seeking to share such images. In many cases, these same platforms that enable further reach to broader networks also constrain not only which images come to prominence or are excluded, but also influence the aesthetic of the images themselves. While earlier scholarship tended to associate the internet with liberty and personal autonomy, beyond commercial and state interference, current research acknowledges that content censorship is an increasingly pervasive, complex and central component of contemporary internet use (e.g. Deibert and Rohozinski 2010, Deibert et al 2011, Dick 2012; Keremoğlu and Weidmann 2020). This continues to spur debates about the freedom of expression as well as about the spreading of images that are misinformative, pose a security risk or transgress the privacy of the individuals depicted.

The chapters in this section study the push-and-pull relationship between the images themselves and the various platform infrastructural dynamics, which in intricate ways decide what is shown, in what way, and what is excluded from conflict representations. They also point to the inherent incongruity that runs throughout these spaces for image dissemination. The chapter by Jun Liu studies content deletion on the Chinese social media platform Sina Weibo, examining the censorship of multimedia posts from the 2014 Umbrella Movement in Hong Kong, also known as the "Occupy Central Movement". In his comparison of censored and uncensored Weibo posts (i.e. posts which have "survived openly"), Liu scrutinise the increasing agility and technological evolution of image censorship practices.

Liu's study underscores the relentless, systematic erasure of "contentious" images from protest events by Chinese authorities, in which top-down regulatory policies depend on both automated and manual content moderation. These content moderation processes at the platform level specifically target visual content, influencing image production practices as well as workarounds to image deletion on the platform. Liu's findings reveal that images depicting highly recognisable protest elements, such as the yellow umbrella from Hong Kong's pro-democracy movement, suffer more intense censorship. Moreover, the systematic image censorship programme on Chinese social media demonstrates deliberate involvement by China's regime to distract people from collective action and political mobilisation, by equally deleting positive- and negative-leaning image content.

The way in which platform logics and policies influence online images from conflicts is further highlighted in Ally McCrow-Young's chapter, which studies post-conflict image-sharing by Instagram users in response to the 2017 Manchester Arena attack. Through an analysis of images from the day immediately following the terror attack, the chapter investigates how Instagram's affordances, its vernacular user cultures and commercial imperatives significantly influence how public expressions of tribute and mourning are framed after such violent attacks. While images from conflicts, particularly those that come to prominence in news media, are often associated with motifs of suffering and of the spectacular and violent, McCrow-Young's chapter sheds critical light on the little-acknowledged circumstance that the everyday perspective is salient to much conflict imagery. The convergence of diverse and mundane topics on Instagram that draw on, for example, fandom and influencer cultures, contributes significantly to how conflict events are experienced on social media, even if they do not normally capture the attention of legacy news media in their coverage of these events. Findings by McCrow-Young suggest that a result of this mingling of affective violent events with vernacular image practices on social media risk diluting and distracting from grief expressions. Additionally, the potential for users to co-opt the publicity of global crises to increase their own visibility is amplified in a space such as Instagram, whose architecture requires specific practices for indexing and engagement.

The complexity of today's social media platforms and their role in shaping conflict imagery underscores that reflexive, and hybrid, methodological approaches to studying these contexts are required. Concluding the volume, Christina Neumayer and Luca Rossi take a forward-looking approach in their chapter, arguing for the need for further reflection on scholarly use of machine learning as a method of analysing images from conflicts. They propose a conceptual framework for tracing how computer vision learns to *see*, by acknowledging the technological, epistemological and human dimensions of computer vision. Addressing the "luring solution" of adopting computational methods in response to the shortcomings of manual analyses, Neumayer and Rossi pose critical questions about the ability of computer vision to adequately capture the multifaceted and contextual research agendas at stake in studying images from conflict. For instance, does computer vision have the depth beyond the descriptive to fully interrogate multifaceted notions such as violence, symbolism or iconicity within images?

All of the chapters in this section remind us to consider the human element of computational methods, underscoring the importance of a mixed method approach. They point to the rich and contextual nature of image content itself, which requires a manual complement to automated methods. The chapter by Liu as well as the one by Neumayer and Rossi's consider the use of image recognition in the study of protest imagery, highlighting the limitation in automated analyses of multimedia data collection and analysis. While quantitative methods and computational developments provide valuable insights about social media images from conflicts, such approaches can also fall short in illuminating the dimensional richness of multimedia visuals. As platforms themselves continue to evolve, scholarly methods must also adapt to these environments, in order to deepen our understanding of how user images are disseminated, shaped and influence contemporary conflict events.

Conclusion: The Interplay of Actors, Images and Platforms

This volume underscores the contradictions and tensions inherent in the rapid growth and prominence of visual content on social media, and the reconfiguration of today's news circuit when it comes to conflict events. Amidst the optimism and amplifying potential of social media images to empower citizens, activists and others to document conflicts in their local areas, they also present a new set of challenges. The context of social media platforms, including their policies and (performative, personal, commercial) vernacular cultures, present additional necessities for verification, spawning new roles for actors involved in conflicts. Issues related to veracity and economic incentives are seemingly at odds with social media's foregrounding of the personal and the emotional.

As we see across chapters in this volume, users respond to different conflicts by taking and sharing images that are performed through the common styles and conventions of social media, and, vice versa, these styles and conventions morph and change through their interaction with conflict events and user engagement. Understanding these varied performances and self-performances in terms of social platform conventions highlights the fact that there is a certain amount of elasticity when it comes to conflict images. This further muddies the water of how we navigate proximity and distance, where hybrid visual genres are a form of creative expression, but also add falsities, such as misinformation and propaganda, masquerading as fact.

To untangle the complexities of social media images and conflict, we have here treated actors, images and platforms separately. Yet, it should be accentuated that the interplay between these three perspectives ultimately conditions and forms our access to experiencing and gathering information about conflicts via visual social media. The precarity and proximity often involved in producing social media images from conflict areas; the interpretive gap between realism and performativity; and the commercial, cultural, political and legislative drivers behind the infrastructures of social media interact in multiple ways that, taken together, present a certain, mediated view of conflicts.

Bibliography

Allan, S. 2013. *Citizen Witnessing: Revisioning Journalism in Times of Crisis*. Cambridge: Polity Press.

Allan, S. and B. Zelizer. 2004. *Reporting War: Journalism in Wartime*. New York: Routledge.

Andén-Papadopoulos, K. and M. Pantti, eds. 2011. *Amateur Images and Global News*. Bristol: Intellect Press.

Andén-Papadopoulos, K. and M. Pantti, eds. 2013. "Re-Imagining Crisis Reporting: Professional Ideology of Journalists and Citizen Eyewitness Images." *Journalism* 14, no. 7: 960–977.

Baym, N. K. 2015. "Connect with Your Audience! The Relational Labor of Connection." *The Communication Review* 18, no. 1: 14–22.

Blaagaard, B. B. and N. G. Mollerup. 2021. "On Political Street Art as Expressions of Citizen Media in Revolutionary Egypt." *International Journal of Cultural Studies* 24, no. 3: 434–453.

Boltanski, L. 1999. *Distant Suffering: Morality, Media and Politics*. Cambridge: Cambridge University Press.

Borger, J., S. Walker, and D. Sabbagh. 2022. "Russia Plans 'Very Graphic' Fake Video as Pretext for Ukraine Invasion, US Claims." *Guardian*, February 3.

Boudana, S., P. Frosh, and A. A. Cohen. 2017. "Reviving Icons to Death: When Historic Photographs Become Digital Memes." *Media, Culture & Society* 39, no. 8: 1210–1230.

Burgess, J. 2006. "Hearing Ordinary Voices: Cultural Studies, Vernacular Creativity and Digital Storytelling." *Continuum* 20, no. 2: 201–214.

Castells, M. 2012. *Networks of Outrage and Hope, Social Movements in the Internet Age*. Cambridge: Polity Press.

Chouliaraki, L. 2006. *The Spectatorship of Suffering*. London: Sage.

Chouliaraki, L. and M. Mortensen. 2022. "Flesh Witnessing: Smartphones, UGC and Embodied Testimony." *Journalism* 23, no 3: 591–598.

Cottle, S. 2008. "'Mediatized Rituals': A Reply to Couldry and Rothenbuhler." *Media, Culture & Society* 30, no. 1: 135–140.

Deibert, R., J. Palfrey, R. Rohozinski, and J. Zittrain, eds. 2011. *Access Contested: Security, Identity, and Resistance in Asian Cyberspace*. Cambridge: The MIT Press.

Deibert, R. and R. Rohozinski. 2010. "Liberation vs. Control: The Future of Cyberspace." *Journal of Democracy* 21, no. 4: 43–57.

Dick, A. L. 2012. "Established Democracies, Internet Censorship and the Social Media Test." *Information Development* 28, no. 4: 259–260.

Eder, J. and C. Klonk, 2017. "'Introduction'. In *Image Operations*, edited by J. Eder and C. Klonk, 1–22. Manchester: Manchester University Press.

Gade, S. 2018. "The Promise of the Index in Contemporary Documentary Performance." *The Nordic Journal of Aesthetics* 27, no. (55–56): 41–64.

Gibbs, M., J. Meese, M. Arnold, B. Nansen, and M. Carter. 2014. "#Funeral and Instagram: Death, Social Media, and Platform Vernacular." *Information, Communication & Society* 18, no. 3: 255–268.

Harding, L. 2022. "'Dumb and Lazy': The Flawed Films of Ukrainian 'Attacks' Made by Russia's 'Fake Factory.'" *Guardian*, February 21.

hooks, bell. 2015. *Black Looks: Race and Representation*. New York: Routledge.

Hutchby, I. 2001. "Technologies, Texts and Affordances." *Sociology* 35, no. 2: 441–456.

Jenkins, H., S. Shresthova, L. Gamber-Thompson, N. Kligler-Vilenchik, A. M. Zimmerman, and E. Soep. 2016. *By Any Media Necessary, the New Youth Activism*. New York: New York University Press.

Jones, M. O. 2021. *Digital Authoritarianism in the Middle East: Deception, Disinformation and Social Media*. London: Hurst.

Keremoğlu, E. and N. B. Weidmann. 2020. "How Dictators Control the Internet: A Review Essay." *Comparative Political Studies* 53, no. (10–11): 1690–1703.

Khamis, S. and K. Vaughn. 2012. "'We Are All Khaled Said': The Potentials and Limitations of Cyberactivism in Triggering Public Mobilization and Promoting Political Change." *Journal of Arab & Muslim Media Research* 4, no. 2: 145–163.

Klinger, U. and J. Svensson. 2014. "The Emergence of Network Media Logic in Political Communication: A Theoretical Approach." *New Media & Society* 17, no. 8: 1241–1257.

Leaver, T. and T. Highfield. 2018. "Visualising the Ends of Identity: Pre-birth and Post-Death on Instagram." *Information, Communication & Society* 21, no. 1: 30–45.

Licoppe, C. and Z. Smoreda. 2005. "Are Social Networks Technologically Embedded?" *Social Networks* 27, no. 4: 317–35.

Liu, J. and J. Zhao. 2021. "More Than Plain Text: Censorship Deletion in the Chinese Social Media." *Journal of the Association for Information Science and Technology* 72, no. 1: 18–31.

Madenga, F. 2021. "From Transparency to Opacity: Storytelling in Zimbabwe under State Surveillance and the Internet Shutdown." *Information, Communication & Society* 24, no. 3: 400–421.

McCrow-Young, A. 2020. "Incongruent Images: Connective Mourning Rituals on Instagram Following the 2017 Manchester Arena Attack: PhD Dissertation." University of Copenhagen, Department of Communication.

Mollerup, N. G. and M. Mortensen. 2020. "Proximity and Distance in the Mediation of Suffering: Local Photographers in War-Torn Aleppo and the International Media Circuit." *Journalism* 21, no. 6: 729–745.

Mortensen, M. 2015. *Journalism and Eyewitness Images: Digital Media, Participation, and Conflict*. New York: Routledge.

Mortensen, M. 2017. "Constructing, Confirming, and Contesting Icons: The Alan Kurdi Imagery Appropriated by #humanitywashedashore, Ai Weiwei, and Charlie Hebdo." *Media, Culture & Society* 39, no. 8: 1142–1161.

Mortensen, M. and C. Neumayer. 2021. "The Playful Politics of Memes." *Information, Communication & Society* 24, no. 16: 2367–2377.

Mottahedeh, N. 2015. *iranelection: Hashtag Solidarity and the Transformation of Online Life*. Palo Alto: Stanford University Press.

Ngoshi Hazel, T. 2021. "Repression, Literary Dissent and the Paradox of Censorship in Zimbabwe." *Journal of Southern African Studies* 47, no. 5: 799–715.

Nowak, J. 2021. "That Prodigious Machinery Designed to Exclude." In *Politics of Disinformation: The Influence of Fake News on the Public Sphere*, edited by P. Bella, G. Lopez-Garcia, E. Campos-Dominguez, P. Masip, and D. Palau-Sampio, 146–158. Hoboken: Wiley-Blackwell.

Olesen, T. 2018. "Memetic Protest and the Dramatic Diffusion of Alan Kurdi." *Media, Culture & Society* 40, no. 5: 656–672.

Papachirissi, Z. 2015. *Affective Publics: Sentiment, Technology, and Politics*. New York: Oxford University Press.

Ratta, D. D. 2021. "Shooting 2011–2021." *Film Quarterly* 75, no. 2: 68–75.

Rogers, R. and S. Niederer. 2020. *The Politics of Social Media Manipulation*. Amsterdam: Amsterdam University Press.

Sekula, A. 1986. "The Body and the Archive." *October* 39, (Winter): 3–64.

Shirky, C. 2008. *Here Comes Everybody, the Power of Organisation without Organisations*. New York: Penguin.

Tagg, J. 1988. *The Burden of Representation: Essays on Photographies and Histories*. Basingstoke: Macmillan Education.

Van Dijck, J. and T. Poell. 2013. "Understanding Social Media Logic." *Media and Communication* 1, no. 1: 2–14.

Wahl-Jorgensen, K. 2015. "Resisting Epistemologies of User-Generated Content?: Cooptation, Segregation and the Boundaries of Journalism." In *Boundaries of Journalism: Professionalism, Practices and Participation*, edited by M. Carlson and S. C. Lewis, 169–185. London: Routledge.

Yazbeck, N. 2021. "Behind the Byline: The Human Toll of How We (Still) Get News out of Syria." *Columbia Journalism Review*, June 16.

Zhukova, E. 2022. "Image Substitutes and Visual Fake History: Historical Images of Atrocity of the Ukrainian Famine 1932–1933 on Social Media." *Visual Communication* 21, 1: 3-27.

1

RELATIONAL LABOUR OR DIGITAL RESISTANCE

Social Media Practices of Non-Western
Women Photographers

Saumava Mitra and Brenda Witherspoon

It is widely understood that the rise of social media has profoundly changed how images of conflicts and crises come to be produced, circulated and consumed by globally dispersed audiences (Mortensen 2015; Blaagaard et al. 2017; Allan 2017). Within this broader area, studies focused on non-Western contexts have investigated images produced by citizen journalists, amateurs and activists that reach global audiences through uptake of their digital content by journalists (e.g. Mortensen 2015; Allan 2017). However, studies on the experiences and practices of *professional* non-Western visual journalists and photographers from places where indirect – structural and cultural – violence is endemic (Galtung and Fischer 2013) or in conflict-affected contexts where direct violence persists (Galtung and Fischer 2013) are only more recently being undertaken (Walsh 2020; Mitra 2020; Mollerup and Mortensen 2020; Zhang and Hadland 2021). In this chapter, we add to this growing academic endeavour by applying a gender-based approach to investigating professional photojournalistic practices and interactions with social media in non-Western contexts. In particular, we explore (a) how social media are perceived by non-Western women photographers as a part of their professional lives and (b) whether they see social media as a platform to circulate alternative images that challenge established regimes of visibility of the peoples and places they photograph.

Digitalisation and Its Impacts on Photographic Labour

Growing digitalisation of the photographic profession has resulted in loss of income security for professional visual journalists and photographers. This is fuelled by unauthorised use of their work without remuneration (Hadland and Barnett 2018a, 6), contractual and freelance labour replacing long-term employment (Thomson 2018; Hadland and Barnett 2018b) and growing use of user-generated images for journalistic purposes that started a process of replacing professionals

DOI: 10.4324/9781003176923-2

(Daubs 2016) and now challenges the very conception of professional identity among photojournalists (Ferrucci et al. 2020). The use of both ad hoc labour and user-generated images is most prominent when it comes to photographing conflicts, crises and other indirect violence-affected contexts outside the West (Mast and Hanegreefs 2015; Mortensen 2015; Istek 2017; Krajewski and Ekdale 2017; Mollerup and Mortensen 2020; Mitra 2020).

Within this context, Thomson (2018) has drawn attention to how digitally mediated interactions with peers and higher-ups have replaced traditional workplace interactions for visual journalists. This importance of digitally mediated networking extends to professional photographers' need to be present and foster relationships on social media for professional purposes: a practice where every fan or follower is viewed as a potential advocate of their work, if not a potential client (Chan 2011, 227).

In what is essentially a gig economy for visual journalists and documentary photographers, promoting themselves professionally through relationships on social media has become necessary but unpaid, immaterial labour. Following Baym's (2015; 2018) description of the online labour of intimate connection-building on social media by music professionals, we use the term "relational labour" (Baym 2015, 16–17; Baym 2018, 16–22) to describe this form of work. In this conceptualisation, broadcasting information, seeking validation from peers and higher-ups, sparking conversations and even maintaining genuine friendships on social media are forms of self-promotion and together make up the relational labour undertaken by creative professionals (Baym 2018, 20).

Relational Labour of Visual Journalists and Photographers

When it comes to social media practices related to journalists' work, much is known about how the lines between personal and professional are blurred in such practices (Ottovordemgentschenfelde 2017; Brems et al. 2017; Molyneux et al. 2018). Unrecognised emotional labour routinely performed by journalists has also been studied for quite some time (see Kotisova 2019 for an overview). Our focus on relational labour of visual journalists and documentary photographers extends these two investigative areas. Firstly, we understand visual journalists and photographers' practices holistically with their personal *and* professional motivations having become inseparable as they, within the context of a gig economy, must connect on social media, while always eyeing the need to monetise these connections (Baym 2015, 16; cf. Chan 2011). The relational labour on social media performed by photographers has been acknowledged (Blaagaard et al. 2017, 1112) or implied (Borges-Rey 2015, 587), but not termed as such, even though the growing need to have an engaged and engaging presence on social media for photographers maintained through image sharing as well as related performative discourses is well known (Borges-Rey 2015; Thomson 2018).

There is evidence, however, that, for visual journalists and photographers, such relational labour on social media gravitates to platforms whose primary affordance is visibility (Laestadius 2017). Recent quantitative data collected worldwide show Facebook, and increasingly Instagram, as the social media of choice for professional photographers (Hadland and Barnett 2018a, 9). Most compellingly for our framework of relational labour, maintaining visibility on such platforms is known to be associated by photographers globally with increased financial rewards (Hadland and Barnett 2018a, 9). Studies on the perceptions and practices of women photographers from non-Western contexts regarding their social media use, and their relational labour on such platforms, are non-existent (cf. Brems et al. 2017, 444).

The need to understand connection-building on social media by photographers as a gendered practice is underscored by recent studies focusing on journalistic practices that exceed traditional journalistic labour. Thomson (2021) found that, unlike their male colleagues, women photographers tend to feel "compelled to stay connected to their subjects post-publication" (p. 969). Mesmer and Jahng's recent study (2021) reinforces Thomson's findings about the emotional labour performed by women journalists and highlights the role social media can play in this context. These point to gender-based variations within extra-journalistic labour performed by photographers and journalists.

At a structural level, Somerstein (2020) found that continuing patterns of gender-based marginalisation effectively render women invisible within the photographic profession. She concludes that such, "… professional invisibility complicates women's access and relationships with other photographers, subjects, authorities, and clients" (p. 683). Somerstein (2021) also notes that, apart from gender, racial dimensions exacerbate such invisibility (p. 8). According to Daniella Zalcman, photojournalist and founder of Women Photograph, an organisation seeking to empower women photographers from under-represented communities around the world, the lack of inclusivity in the industry stems from intersectional – both gender-related and racial – marginalisation. As she said in an interview with Tim Greyhavens (2017):

> When an industry is largely populated by white men, generally speaking, the people they tend to reach out to, to mentor, are people who remind them of them when they were younger. So white men are mentoring young white men instead of people of color or young women.

The *outcome* of what Somerstein found in her studies (2020; 2021), and what Zalcman has observed as a professional and seeks to remedy as an activist, is most likely reflected in Hadland and Barnett's findings (2018a) that a non-Caucasian, non-male photographer from outside North America and Europe is more likely than their peers to experience financial precarity. Importantly, the lack of ability to foster relationships through geographical and cultural proximity to powerful "image-brokers" in the international photography industry situated in Western countries (Gürsel 2016) further increases the need to maintain professional visibility and relationships through social media for women photographers in non-Western countries (Zalcman, personal communication, 20 May 2021).

Thus, we argue for a need to focus on the relational labour of non-Western women photographers on social media. As freelancification has increased and digitally mediated relationships between editors, audiences and photographers have become the norm, these women are the most likely to experience intersectional marginalisation because of their gender, ethnicity and geocultural positionalities, and thus have the most motivation to engage in this form of relational labour. Based on this, our first research goal in this study is:

> *What are the perceptions among non-Western women photographers regarding social media platforms' role in their professional lives?*

The Potential of Social Media to Offer Alternative Visual Expressions

Rich theoretical and conceptual discussions, as well as empirical evidence, have shed light on the "pictorial hegemony" (Campbell 2009, 54) underpinned by a "visual economy" (ibid) that organises peoples, places and knowledge structures implicated in the production, circulation and reception of images in ways that are based on current economic, political and cultural power dynamics at local, regional and global levels (Campbell 2009, 53). When seen from a contemporary transnational perspective, this hegemony has created "regimes of visibility" (Chouliaraki and Stolic 2017) that govern how peoples and places outside the West come to be represented for Western audiences, especially with visual representation of conflicts and crises.

Social media's potential to circumvent or conform to these established regimes of visibility has been much studied in the context of their particular affordances. While Dencik and Allan (2017, 1186) found "social media platforms are being tested to find new possibilities for the visualisation of crises, often privileging creative and unconventional types of truth-telling to advance human-centred narratives otherwise difficult to align with news agendas", Blaagaard et al. (2017, 1114) have questioned "whether the options that digital media make available for actors involved in conflict to represent their experiences and perspectives genuinely challenge implicit and explicit hierarchies of visibility".[1] In sum, social media's ability to foster alternative visualisations of distant peoples and places provides grounds for both optimism and pessimism when it comes to challenging the well-known problems in how distant conflicts and crises are represented for globally dispersed audiences.

But the potential agency of professionals who produce and circulate such visuals, particularly those outside Western contexts, to *challenge* these established regimes of visibility *from within* has not been significantly investigated. We argue that it is important to investigate the perceptions and practices of professional photographers, who are also affected by the conflicts and crises they photograph, when it comes to using social media to offer alternative visual expressions. While they are driven to acquire "the cultural and social status to be seen and heard" (Blaagaard et al. 2017,

1114) by harnessing social media as visual journalists and photographers working within "corporate structures of media institutions", their positionality at the margins of these structures has the potential to make them active agents in challenging the established regimes of visibility as well (Blaagaard et al. 2017, 1114–1115). Based on this, the second research goal of this study is:

> *Are social media seen as having the potential, and harnessed as such by non-Western women photographers, to circulate alternative images that challenge established regimes of visual representation regarding the places and peoples affected by direct and indirect violence that they photograph?*

Methodology

Between March and May 2020, we conducted semi-structured online interviews with 20 female-identifying photographers who described their work as falling within or encompassing photojournalism, documentary photography, visual journalism and, in one case, visual art (cf. Hadland et al. 2015, 15). All were members of Native Agency and/or Women Photograph – organisations representing professional photographers from under-represented communities outside the West and of marginalised gender identities, respectively. Both maintain online member databases which allowed us to invite participants. The photographers' identities and countries are confidential under the study's ethical protocols; broadly they identified as from 17 non-Western countries from South Asia (5 photographers), South-East Asia (5), Sub-Saharan Africa (4), Middle East and North Africa (3) and Latin America and the Caribbean (3).

These countries host fragile democracies or politically repressive regimes that rank mid-to-low on indicators measuring democracy. Almost all feature low on gender-equity indicators and high on incidences of gender-based violence. Besides these forms of structural and cultural violence, all but four countries (three of which previously have had large-scale, multiyear, intrastate wars) are also affected by direct violence tied to ongoing state-based or non-state-based conflicts. We take a grounded approach (Charmaz 2005) in interpreting the interview data and report the statements of the photographers relevant to their perceptions of and practices on social media directly rather than through intermediary interpretative codes.

Social Media Content Analysis

We qualitatively analysed social media content these photographers shared as well. Comparability with the interview data through maintaining a qualitative focus informed our "small data" approach in this area (Mayr and Weller 2017). While all 20 photographers have active Instagram profiles, only some used Facebook and Twitter. As such, we focused on Instagram for better comparability, as different platforms' affordances differ and can determine user behaviour (Laestadius 2017). We collected Instagram posts starting approximately a year before the interviews.

This pre-Covid-19 timeframe made the social media data more comparable to the interviews because the pandemic did not feature significantly in interviewees' responses in the first half of 2020. Instagram posting frequency differed among the photographers, so our data collection parameter was the first ten posts by each in 2019. As such, our analysis is based on 200 Instagram posts, a number manageable to analyse individually with a qualitative focus. We limited our analysis to primary posts, not comments or other user engagements, because the photographers themselves were our focus. We did analyse hashtags the photographers used in primary posts to understand the connections they intended to build and the contexts they wanted to suggest (Laestadius 2017, 578).

The posts were analysed multi-modally, taking into account both the images posted and accompanying written texts and hashtags. Based on the unfixed (visual) and fixed (textual) meanings embedded in these posts (Laestadius 2017), five categories were identified – personal, promotional, political, alternative views and exotica. Individual posts were understood to fall within multiple categories.

Two categories were defined based primarily on understandings of relational labour, as well as previous studies on journalists' use of social media.

> *Personal:* Posts related to family members, friends, leisure activities including travel where no photographic assignment or other professional work is mentioned. The photographer herself is not mentioned textually or present visually.
>
> *Promotional:* Visual or textual references to the photographer's self. Posts that showcase photographic and journalistic skills, e.g. visually or textually highlighting aesthetic composition and editing or by highlighting news-related event/issue/actor photographed. Posts with textual highlighting of camera equipment used and genre of photography. Posts mentioning assignment or work-related travel or self-led photographic projects, or with images presented as outtakes from photographic work. Posts textually referring to the photographer's Instagram followers.

Two other categories were informed by theoretical and empirical understandings of photographic representations of conflicts and crises-affected places and peoples in non-Western contexts (see Mitra et al. 2021b for a full discussion).

> *Political:* Visual or textual references to social or political upheaval, humanitarian crisis, direct and indirect violence in the photographer's own country and neighbouring region. References to electoral politics or to gender and other forms of discrimination, marginalisation or repression were understood to be part of this category.
>
> *Alternative View:* Visual or textual *claims* to show or refer to photographer's country's or neighbouring region's politics (understood broadly as in the category immediately above), peoples and places in a novel way through implicit

or explicit inter-textual references to existing regimes of visual representation. Such claims were most often embedded through hashtags. The most common form these took were #Everyday[country/region/continent].

Another code was also informed by theoretical and empirical understandings of photographic representations of conflicts and crises-affected places and peoples, and of non-Western contexts more broadly, but was unique in being unexpected based on the interview data.

> *Exotica:* Posts that visually or textually reinforced pictorial hegemony through established tropes and stereotypes associated with the peoples and places of countries or regions. We restricted this code to posts by the photographer about and from countries they did not self-identify with.

Relational Labour of Women Photographers on Social Media

The women photographers interviewed for this study largely perceived social media as instrumental in gaining and maintaining visibility within the industry. For one photographer from South Asia, this view was supported by her direct experience when moving into her role as a professional photojournalist:

> It was more of a hobby. … I also took pictures, and I shared them on my Facebook. And a friend of mine re-shared it, and an editor at a daily newspaper in [home country] picked up those pictures and asked me if they could publish them in the newspaper, and they gave me more than half a page. So when I saw my pictures published for the first time, that's when I realised that this is what I want to do from now on.

The photographers also perceived social media as essential at subsequent stages of career progression. According to them, it helped in advancing their career and moving from working in national media industries in their own countries to working transnationally for international media organisations centred in Western countries. As a photographer from Sub-Saharan Africa explained,

> It is thanks to social networks because a lot of the contracts that I have, be they from Instagram, from tweeting, good contacts, [are] always through social networks. Therefore, it is thanks in part to what I showed, what I write, that validates me a bit and that made me known at the international level. I would say that is often [the] case with social networks. … It's a bit like professional accounts for me, not just for social networks, for hobbies; no, it's professional. Facebook [is] also professional. [Translated from French]

Beyond entering and gaining international visibility in their profession, some described social media as key to maintaining professional networks. The need to remain visible, among peers, colleagues, editors and audiences required constant relational labour, said a photographer from Southeast Asia.

> A lot of it, I feel, is true word of mouth and constant, constant, constant networking, which you actually have to do. And really putting yourself out there in the in the digital space, like in Instagram or on Facebook or, you know, constantly updating people, what you're working on, that sort of help them to remember that, OK, I know this person in [home country] whom I could possibly get to work on these issues or travel in Southeast Asia.

Interviewees often mentioned using social media for relational labour in the context of disadvantages based on gender, ethnicity and their geocultural positionality away from the West. As such, they associated their need to build and maintain visibility through social media with their need to transcend the gendered, racialised and geocultural exclusions they faced as non-Western women photographers. Several mentioned that they were advised by established professionals in their line of work to engage in relational labour on social media. A participant from South Asia cited this as a formal goal during an international professional mentorship programme, while another from the same region said learning how to harness hashtags on Instagram for promotional purposes was part of her mentorship experience as well.

> I am very, very bad at updating my Instagram, so I made a promise to them, my mentors, that I'm going to be better. And always making a note of that, and you know, trying to post more on Instagram.
>
> Our mentorship programme is not only like, goes through our work, mentoring of work. There are other things also, to manage our website, for example, and how to be active on the Everyday [hashtag], like how to manage Instagram.

The photographers emphasised that other photographers from their countries or regions, particularly women, needed to also recognise the potential of social media in this respect and engage in relational labour on these platforms to gain visibility. As a photographer from Southeast Asia described,

> White reporters, white photographers, are still much more visible here than locals because [of] the[ir] contacts and editors look out for [them], particularly because they just are more visible on social media, for example. … I also remember that my mentor also sometimes like at one point just told me that, you know, sometimes it's really difficult for them to find a woman photographer in the area, simply because you know they're not on social media, for example. They're not visible and this kind of thing.

Apart from relational labour focused on professional advancement through increased visibility among editors and audiences, photographers cited social media in the context of maintaining supportive connections with peers. Some described such networks as valuable in a non-monetary sense, such as this photographer from South Asia, who sought to understand other national contexts through other photographers' social media accounts:

> There are so many people there sharing their experience there, their problem there, so many things. That also helps us like what is happening over there. We also understand what is happening globally.

But such peer networks were not perceived as fully separated from the motive of monetising connections built on social media. As two women from the Middle East/North Africa described:

> There's a Facebook group we're all on. Anyone who has questions can just go in and pop in their question and can be answered. It can be a very detailed question about like a fee or a certain grant that is being opened and you want to apply for and you need certain paperwork for it, which you don't have.

> So this community and network really helps me to push further, to learn, to open, to ask. … Like assignments, sorry I didn't know about th[ese] things [laughs], like pitching story to magazines, like doing money from websites, like a lot of things that I didn't know. So this community is really, really helping me out.

However, the interviewees also recognised the limits of networking via social media compared with in-person connections. Two photographers from South Asia and from Sub-Saharan Africa, respectively, spoke to the shortcomings of digitally mediated social interactions and the possibility that such connections are less robust compared with real-world interactions:

> Obviously, it's helpful, but it's not as good as when you are connecting people really in a very personal way, not in a virtual way.

> I knew others based on like, OK, we follow each other. But it was hard to … convert the follows and the Instagram likes into relationships.

Notwithstanding, we found that social media were integral to how the photographers managed their professional lives. This was directly linked to their view that social media could transform their comparative lack of visibility in the profession, particularly transnationally. Relational labour required of women photographers in non-Western contexts finds a powerful home in social media, according to them, particularly on image-driven platforms Facebook and Instagram, despite some limitations.

Photographers' Perception of Social Media as Platforms for Alternative Visuals

Many women we interviewed also saw social media as tools for resisting what they see as misrepresentation of peoples and places. In general, these photographers' professional perceptions and practices were highly marked by their awareness about and reaction against the iniquitous nature of regimes of visibility when it came to the people and places they photographed but also felt they belonged to. Almost all of the women interviewed reflected on the history and practice of photojournalism misrepresenting non-Western societies by visually over-emphasising societal problems, conflicts and crises over other aspects of life, which they saw largely continuing at present. They mentioned the lack of respect for non-Western peoples as photographic subjects compared with those in the West both during the act of creating images and through the images themselves.

All 20 women also saw their roles as professional visual journalists or photographers to include actively resisting entrenched tropes, stereotypes and disrespectful practices through the images they produce as well as how they produce them. The perceptions about their professional role and practice as non-Western women photographers were marked by an intersectional reflexivity. They perceived a goal of challenging and changing established regimes of visibility accorded to the peoples and places they had close ties with.

When it came to social media as a platform to exercise such intersectional reflexivity, the photographers were more ambivalent about their potential to offer alternative visual expressions. Several spoke specifically to social media as amplifying existing tropes and stereotypes at times, such as this photographer from Southeast Asia and another from the Middle East and North Africa:

> So, people actually want to see what they want to see. And all they want to see is very beautiful images, but not necessarily true. ... So that ... constant exoticising of places, I feel like I see that every day.

> It bothers me that there are stories of starvation. I mean, the starving baby now, all what do you see when you open like just write the hashtag [home country] and Twitter. And that's what's the first thing you would see. But there are so many good work[s] that ha[ve] emerged, you know, to tackle this issue ... And yet this is not what you're going to see in the media.

However, the photographers did not link their own image-sharing practices with such pessimistic views of social media's potential to offer alternative visual expressions. When it came to their own ability to offer alternative representations, including on social media, they were confident in their intention, and ability, to challenge the established regimes of visibility, as these two photographers from Southeast Asia and from Sub-Saharan Africa, respectively, mentioned:

But it's just in the past two years that I have realised like, oh, my God, I'm the only [minority] female photographer. And it's so important to try my best to push those issues out there. I guess it really helps with social media to actually have that space because in our country we do a lot of talking about this and a lot of things. … I'm starting to try to push those issues out there and engage in those conversations. Because I am a minority myself. So I feel that there's so much of things which needs to be discussed, and I feel like this great responsibility to bring it forward.

It's so that we can fight [misrepresentation] on our social networks, on our sites. … It's not just war. There is another choice. … if you see a little on my Instagram account, it's scenes of everyday life, of populations from everywhere I go because I have a bit of the chance to travel in several regions from my country. I kind of capture everything I see, everything that goes to my head, everything I feel, everything I see, everything that is happening around me – a little to promote my region, but also to show the daily life of these people. [Translated from French]

A photographer from the Middle East and North Africa said offering such alternative visuals clearly fell within her professional role: "I feel like I'm not an activist necessarily, but I have a role to educate, and I'm going to take that".

Some photographers we interviewed bemoaned the use of their images in traditional publications with inaccurate captions, either as initially written by others during editing or when the photos were repurposed months or years later to illustrate unrelated events. Social media offered them a chance at reclamation by writing text to accompany the images and thus fix the meanings they wanted to convey. In this context, a photographer from Sub-Saharan Africa mentioned the hashtag adoptions and extensions introduced by Everyday Everywhere, the Instagram page of the Everyday Project, a collective started by two photographers seeking to challenge accepted representations of people and places outside the West in international media.[2] She described what she saw as the value of this project:

[It offers] a common vision, but behind, the objective, it is to break the stigmas [that are] in each region. For example, in my area, there is war and all … [and] the other side people are not used to seeing. … Everyone can value their region as they wish. I do that on my page. … You have an Instagram page and a Facebook page and a Twitter page; that's where you can share all that you have to share. … You… can show, for example, beautiful landscapes and fishermen on the lake. A few things [that are] a bit specific. People aren't used to seeing that. [Translated from French]

Among the Instagram posts by these 20 women photographers we analysed, the hashtag #Everyday[country/region/continent] was widely used to contextualise their posts as offering alternative views of their countries and communities. This brings us to analysis of the photographers' social media posts.

Photographers' Use of Instagram for Relational Labour and Providing Alternative Visuals

Table 1.1 shows our findings from the photographers' Instagram posts.

The majority of the Instagram posts we analysed (140 of 200) fell within two or more categories. However, a clear ranking was evident in how the 20 women we interviewed employed Instagram during the period when we collected data. Posts with implicit and explicit promotional motivations, and as such speaking to relational labour, were employed by all 20 photographers and constituted almost 80% of analysed posts. Three-quarters (15) of these photographers sought to promote themselves in at least 90% of their posts. Significantly, the single biggest overlap in categories was between personal and promotional. Of those whose posts included both categories, 14 of 16 had no more than two posts that included one category but not the other, signifying just how blurry the line might be for photographers in the current gig economy. In turn, when seen together with the interviews, this lends further credence that women photographers from non-Western contexts rely on relational labour conducted through social media to gain visibility otherwise not accorded to them.

We found just less than one-third of the 200 posts we analysed (60 out of the 200) included claims to provide an alternative view of peoples and places the

TABLE 1.1 Categories of Interviewees' Instagram Posts (N=200)

	Promotional	Personal	Alternate View	Political	Exotica
Photographer 1	1	0	10	3	0
Photographer 2	10	3	6	0	1
Photographer 3	9	3	0	7	1
Photographer 4	10	10	0	0	10
Photographer 5	2	7	9	1	0
Photographer 6	10	0	9	7	0
Photographer 7	10	8	8	0	0
Photographer 8	9	2	0	0	0
Photographer 9	10	0	0	0	0
Photographer 10	3	8	0	0	0
Photographer 11	5	8	3	0	0
Photographer 12	10	7	5	0	0
Photographer 13	10	2	1	0	0
Photographer 14	10	3	1	4	0
Photographer 15	9	6	0	0	1
Photographer 16	10	0	3	8	0
Photographer 17	10	8	0	0	0
Photographer 18	9	4	4	6	0
Photographer 19	10	4	0	0	0
Photographer 20	1	9	1	0	4
Total by category	**158**	**92**	**60**	**36**	**17**
Photographers with at least one post in category	20	16	12	7	5

photographers had close ties with. This category was the third-largest among the five categories, and a majority of the photographers (12 out of the 20) had at least one such post, while nine had more than three such posts.

The two least present categories were those with overtly political content and those reinforcing stereotypes about countries and regions other than the photographers' own.

Image-Building through Image-Sharing

The women photographers' perception of social media was both utilitarian and, when it came to their own practices, tending towards utopian. They mentioned the platforms as tools to circumvent or transcend the gendered, racialised and geoculturally constituted invisibility imposed upon them within the transnational field of international photography. In sum, based on our interviews and the analysis of Instagram posts, we found that the photographers viewed and most often used social media platforms to conduct relational labour to gain professional visibility, build professional networks with peers and higher-ups and communicate with audiences.

The photographers also saw social media as platforms to offer images of their countries and communities that challenge "pictorial hegemony" (Campbell 2009) and actively seek to change the regimes of visibility (Chouliaraki and Stolic 2017) that are reified by supply and demand in the international photography industry. Our analysis of 200 Instagram posts shows posts that matched this latter category were less present compared with the ubiquity of posts of the former category. However, when seen in relation with the accounts provided during the interviews, the potential of harnessing social media to change and challenge the status quo of how non-Western peoples and places affected by conflicts and crises are represented cannot be entirely discounted.

In this context, it is important to reiterate an interesting question that Blaagaard et al. (2017) have raised:

> New "visibility entrepreneurs" appearing on the scene may to some degree reconfigure the traditional distribution of power inherent in the politics of visibility (i.e. who possesses the cultural and social status as well as the geopolitical situatedness to be seen and heard). Be that as it may, established hierarchies hardly seem to be subverted at this point. Indeed, commercialisation and commodification potentially threatens to hand alternative visual expressions over to the corporate power of media institutions.
>
> *Blaagaard et al. 2017, 1114*

While the term *new visibility entrepreneurs* as used by the authors above is primarily meant for individuals from outside the professional boundaries of visual journalism or photography, our findings show that, within the international photography industry itself, photography professionals whose geopolitical situation and ethnic, cultural and gender identities place them at the margins, even if still within the loci of "corporate power of media institutions", may play a role in reconfiguring traditional power dynamics inherent in the politics of visibility. Indeed, the very forces of commercialisation and commodification that Blaagaard et al. (ibid.) decry might fuel such reconfiguration because the need to be entrepreneurial through relational labour on social media is paramount for these professionals. As a result, promoting themselves as unique through sharing images and associated performative discourses may be especially important. Our analysis indicated that such social media use, if not ubiquitous, may be substantially present among women photographers from non-Western contexts.

This chapter cannot provide a definitive answer regarding non-Western women photographers' relational labour on social media resulting in alternatives to entrenched regimes of visibilities of places and peoples experiencing direct and indirect forms of violence through the images they share given its narrow and qualitative focus. But we argue it points to the *potential* for alternative visual expressions of conflicts and crises to emerge from the convergence of the forces of the current gig economy, social media affordances and the individual motivations and agency of these photographers to promote themselves as professionals who photograph violence-affected societies they hail from.

In sum, our analysis shows a distinct possibility that resistance through alternative visual expression by professional photographers who have been traditionally marginalised can find a foothold in social media, given that they are also driven to build their personas as professionals with a unique insight into the locations where they work. This sometimes takes the form of offering aesthetic resistance through images shared on social media. This question of whether and how the two purposes feed each other – specifically whether substantial visibility is a precursor to successful advancement of alternative images and whether the act of appearing novel or unique, through providing alternative representations on social media, enhances visibility – we argue, merits further investigation. Particularly, the implications for alternative visual expressions to emerge as a result of the professional strategy of image-building through image-sharing on social media for photographers who see themselves as marginalised within the profession needs further exploration through grounded and qualitative investigations.

We have painted a cautiously optimistic picture of the possibility of aesthetic resistance to existing regimes of visibility and the entrenched pictorial hegemony on social media by non-Western women photographers. But we cannot find grounds for such optimism when it comes to overt political engagement or resistance by these photographers. Less than one-fifth (36 out of the 200) of all analysed posts could be interpreted as involving engagement with politics, forms of injustice or oppression by the photographers. While we are not able to provide conclusive evidence regarding this, the relative paucity of Instagram posts of this category may also be linked to the politically repressive contexts within which most of the photographers worked, as well as the heightened potential for online harassment that women journalists experience.

Online presence for journalists in conflict-affected contexts, politically repressive regimes and societies where gender-related inequity and gender-based violence are high is not risk-free, as it increases journalists' surfaces of exposure to potential threat and harassment (Mitra et al. 2021a, 92). Most recent global data show that female journalists as a whole are indeed more likely to face online harassment (Posetti et al. 2021). However, this lack of political engagement might also be linked to the shaping of the photographers' social media use by the overarching market logic inherent in relational labour, as a result of which overt political engagement might be seen as antagonising for potential employers or sections of the audience. The need to maintain journalistic neutrality could be another cause.

Another emergent finding from our analysis was the presence of posts that exoticised peoples and places other than the photographers' own, through posts that resonated with existing tropes and stereotypes. These were the least prevalent of all the categories and found in the posts of only one-quarter of the photographers. A single one of the five photographers with such Instagram posts accounted for 10 of the 17 posts which could be categorised as reinforcing stereotypes. While numerically not very significant within the sample, we believe it is noteworthy that photographers' articulations of promoting alternative views about misrepresented peoples and places were counteracted by the presence also of posts that overlapped with historical stereotypes when it came to *other* peoples and places than their own. Further study drawing on larger samples of social media posts by a larger number of photographers would be needed before any firm conclusions can be drawn regarding this, however.

More broadly, we hope this chapter will help refocus academic research agenda on social media and conflict images to have a more globally inclusive perspective of visual professionals whose practices need to be investigated in ways that keep in view the particular positionalities they occupy within their profession.

Acknowledgement: The authors wish to thank doctoral students Sara Creta and Rabia Qusien, and Dr Andreas Rauh of Dublin City University, as well as Neysa Goodman of Iowa State University and independent researcher Stephanie McDonald, for their assistance with this study at several stages.

Notes

1 See also Krajewski and Ekdale (2017) for their study showing the failure of user-generated content-based journalism in producing counter-narratives to existing tropes and stereotypes in the context of a natural disaster.
2 www.instagram.com/theeverydayproject_/?hl=en Link accessed November 18, 2021.

Bibliography

Allan, S., ed. 2017. *Photojournalism and citizen journalism: Co-operation, collaboration and connectivity*. London: Taylor & Francis.

Baym, N. K. 2015. "Connect with your audience! The relational labor of connection." *The communication review* 18, no. 1: 14–22.

Baym, N. K. 2018. *Playing to the crowd: Musicians, audiences, and the intimate work of connection.* New York: New York University Press.

Blaagaard, B., M. Mortensen, and C. Neumayer. 2017. "Digital images and globalized conflict." *Media, Culture & Society* 39, no. 8: 1111–1121.

Borges-Rey, E. 2015. "News images on Instagram: The paradox of authenticity in hyperreal photo reportage." *Digital Journalism* 3, no. 4: 571–593.

Brems, C., M. Temmerman, T. Graham, and M. Broersma. 2017. "Personal branding on Twitter: How employed and freelance journalists stage themselves on social media." *Digital Journalism* 5, no. 4: 443–459.

Campbell, D. 2009. "'Black skin and blood': Documentary photography and santu mofokeng's critique of the visualization of apartheid south Africa." *History and Theory* 48, no. 4: 52–58.

Chan, L. 2011. *Social media marketing for digital photographers.* Hoboken: John Wiley & Sons.

Charmaz, K. 2005. "Grounded theory in the 21st century: A qualitative method for advancing social justice research." In *Handbook of qualitative research*, edited by N. K. Denzin and Y. S. Lincoln, 507–535. Thousand Oaks: Sage.

Chouliaraki, L. and T. Stolic. 2017. "Rethinking media responsibility in the refugee 'crisis': A visual typology of European news." *Media, Culture & Society* 39, no. 8: 1162–1177.

Daubs, M. 2016. "The Social News Network: The appropriation of community labour in CNN's iReport." *The Political Economy of Communication* 3, no. 2: 55–73.

Dencik, L. and S. Allan. 2017. "In/visible conflicts: NGOs and the visual politics of humanitarian photography." *Media, Culture & Society* 39, no. 8: 1178–1193.

Ferrucci, P., R. Taylor, and K. I. Alaimo. 2020. "On the boundaries: Professional photojournalists navigating identity in an age of technological democratization." *Digital Journalism* 8, no. 3: 367–385.

Galtung, J. and D. Fischer. 2013. "Violence: Direct, structural and cultural". In *Johan Galtung: Pioneer of Peace Research*, edited by D. Fischer, 35–40. Berlin: Springer.

Greyhavens, T. 2017. "We Can't Wait Any Longer: An Interview with Daniella Zalcman." *Timgreyhavens.com*, October 30. www.timgreyhavens.com/post/we-can-t-wait-any-lon ger-an-interview-with-daniella-zalcman

Gürsel, Z. D. 2016. *Image brokers: Visualizing world news in the age of digital circulation.* Berkeley: University of California Press.

Hadland, A., D. Campbell, and P. Lambert. 2015. *The state of news photography: The lives and livelihoods of photojournalists in the digital age.* Oxford: Reuters Institute for the Study of Journalism.

Hadland, A. and C. Barnett. 2018a. *The state of news photography: Photojournalists' attitudes toward work practices, technology and life in the digital age.* Sterling: University of Stirling.

Hadland, A. and C. Barnett. 2018b. "The gender crisis in professional photojournalism: Demise of the female gaze?" *Journalism Studies* 19, no. 13: 2011–2020.

Istek, P. 2017. "On their own: Freelance photojournalists in conflict zones." *Visual Communication Quarterly* 24, no. 1: 32–39.

Kotisova, J. 2019. "The elephant in the newsroom: Current research on journalism and emotion." *Sociology Compass* 13, no. 5: 1–11.

Krajewski, J. M. T and B. Ekdale. 2017. "Constructing cholera: CNN iReport, the Haitian cholera epidemic, and the limits of citizen journalism." *Journalism Practice* 11, no. 2–3: 229–246.

Laestadius, L. 2017. "Instagram". In *The SAGE handbook of social media research methods*, edited by L. Sloan and A. Quan-Haase, 573–592. London: Sage.

Mast, J. and S. Hanegreefs. 2015. "When news media turn to citizen-generated images of war: Transparency and graphicness in the visual coverage of the Syrian conflict." *Digital Journalism* 3, no. 4: 594–614.

Mayr, P. and K. Weller. 2017. "Think before you collect: Setting up a data collection approach for social media studies." In *The SAGE handbook of social media research methods*, edited by L. Sloan and A. Quan-Haase, 108–124. London: Sage.

Mesmer, K. and M. R. Jahng. 2021. "Using Facebook to discuss aspects of industry safety: How women journalists enact ethics of care in online professional space." *Journalism Studies* 22, no. 8: 1083–1102.

Mitra, S. 2020. "'Picturing Afghan women' for Western audiences: The Afghan perspective." *Journalism* 21, no. 6: 800–820.

Mitra, S., M. Høiby, and M. Garrido. 2021a. "Medium-specific threats for journalists: Examples from Philippines, Afghanistan and Venezuela." *Journalism Practice* 15, no. 1: 80–98.

Mitra, S., S. Creta, and S. McDonald. 2021b. "How our rage is represented: Acts of resistance among women photographers of the Global South." In *Insights on peace and conflict reporting*, edited by K. Skare Orgeret. 89–105. London: Routledge.

Mollerup, N. G. and M. Mortensen. 2020. "Proximity and distance in the mediation of suffering: Local photographers in war-torn Aleppo and the international media circuit." *Journalism* 21, no. 6: 729–745.

Molyneux, L., A. Holton, and S. C. Lewis. 2018. "How journalists engage in branding on Twitter: Individual, organizational, and institutional levels." *Information, Communication & Society* 21, no. 10: 1386–1401.

Mortensen, M. 2015. *Journalism and eyewitness images: Digital media, participation, and conflict*. London: Routledge.

Ottovordemgentschenfelde, S. 2017. "'Organizational, professional, personal': An exploratory study of political journalists and their hybrid brand on Twitter." *Journalism* 18, no. 1: 64–80.

Posetti, J., N. Shabbir, D. Maynard, K. Bontcheva, and N. Aboulez. 2021. *The chilling: Global trends in online violence against women journalists*. Paris: UNESCO.

Somerstein, R. 2020. "'Stay back for your own safety': News photographers, interference, and the photographs they are prevented from taking." *Journalism* 21, no. 6: 746–765.

Somerstein, R. 2021. "'Just a junior journalist': Field theory and editorial photographers' gendered experiences." *Journalism Practice* 15, no. 5: 669–687.

Thomson, T. J. 2018. "Freelance photojournalists and photo editors: Learning and adapting in a (mostly faceless) virtual world." *Journalism Studies* 19, no. 6: 803–823.

Thomson, T. J. 2021. "Mapping the emotional labor and work of visual journalism." *Journalism* 22, no. 4: 956–973.

Walsh, L. 2020. *Conversations on conflict photography*. London: Routledge.

Zhang, S. I. and A. Hadland. 2021. "A survey of Chinese photojournalists: Identities, work conditions and attitudes in the digital age." In *Chinese news discourse: From perspectives of communication, linguistics and pedagogy*, edited by N. X. Liu, C. Veecock, and S. I. Zhang, 43–61. London: Routledge.

2

THE UNFOLDING OF A PROXY PROFESSION

Evidence, Verification and Human Dignity on Social Media

Sandra Ristovska

Today's social media landscape is full of videos whose meanings are often unclear, among which are various eyewitness videos documenting war and conflict that offer a glimpse into possible human rights claims. Such videos are frequently produced, circulated or used for multiple purposes by activists, bystanders, refugees, journalists, nongovernmental organisations (NGOs), courts, whistleblowers, militaries, law enforcement agents and even terrorist groups. By offering an entry point for witnessing the complex unfolding of global conflicts, eyewitness videos can perform important evidentiary and advocacy functions in the struggles for human rights as illustrated by the Black Lives Matter movement in the US.

Over the last decade, different institutions like journalism, the law and political advocacy have been adjusting their workflows to tap into the evidentiary potential of eyewitness video as a way of offsetting a varied set of cultural, social, techno-logical and financial challenges (Allan 2013; Dubberley et al. 2020; McPherson 2016; Ristovska 2021; Thorsen and Allan 2014; Weizman 2017). For example, the increasing use of eyewitness video in news reporting, criminal investigations and human rights advocacy has been the result of wide-ranging concerns such as journalism's inability to report directly from conflict areas like Syria and Myanmar, the costs associated with witness protection at international criminal courts and tribunals, and the emerging forensic sensibility across law and policy domains. It is not surprising, then, that the institutional and legal turn to eyewitness video has been accompanied by professional concerns about verification standards and mechanisms for assessing such footage.

Various human rights collectives have seized on this moment, turning these institutional and legal challenges into opportunities for human rights practice by seeking to professionalise video activism, defined here as a wide-ranging set of practices in line with Tina Askanius's (2020) framework. The professionalisation efforts, however, have not led to what sociologists identify as professions: occupations

DOI: 10.4324/9781003176923-3

that maintain autonomy over their work and safeguard their specialised knowledge through education, competence tests, licensing procedures and credentials as typically evident in medicine and the law (e.g. Elliott 1972; Larson 1977). Instead, those efforts have resulted in a so-called proxy profession, which uses video as a human rights tool across policy-relevant contexts (Ristovska 2021).

This chapter draws on this prior work on the professionalisation of human rights video activism to illuminate the role and scope of the proxy profession in the mediatisation of global wars and conflicts on social media. It is based on a larger institutional ethnography of human rights collectives like Amnesty International (Amnesty), Human Rights Watch (HRW), Syrian Archive, University of California at Berkeley's Human Rights Center (HRC), WITNESS and others, spanning nine years of research (2012–2021). Human rights collectives is an umbrella term for the diverse range of NGOs, activist groups and research agencies characterising today's human rights field: well-known global organisations like Amnesty and HRW that engage in research, campaigning and advocacy; mid- to small-sized activist groups like WITNESS and Syrian Archive that work primarily with video and new technologies; and university-based research centres like HRC that partner with human rights advocacy groups (for a detailed overview see Ristovska 2021, 2–5). The methodological approach borrows from ethnography by incorporating (1) semi-structured interviews with over 40 staffers working at these human rights collectives in research, campaigning, advocacy and communications units, conducted in-person or online and based on open-ended questions about video's role in human rights work; (2) textual analysis of various organisational publications produced by these collectives, such as documents, reports, books, articles, blog posts and podcasts; as well as (3) personal observations at various conferences and meetings attended by these staffers, including at the NGOs' offices in New York City, Washington DC and London.[1]

Understanding these human rights collectives as proxy professionals sheds light on the practices through which they have been able to claim authority as visual experts, rendering video meaningful as evidence across the institutional calculus supporting human rights. This chapter therefore provides a brief overview of a previous discussion about the development of human rights video activism as a proxy profession and applies it in the context of social media and eyewitness video specifically. It suggests that the proxy professional status enables human rights collectives to promote evidentiary standards, investigative protocols and information policies for eyewitness video, all of which are now taken seriously across decision-making contexts. Yet the proxy profession also confines visual human rights work to institutional and legal logics which can limit eyewitness video's potential to address broader challenges to human dignity around the world.

A Brief Overview of the Proxy Profession

In his examination of the evolving status of professions in Europe and the US throughout the 20th century, Eliot Freidson (2001) used the concept of professionalism to describe "a set of interconnected institutions providing economic support and social organisation that sustains the occupational control of work" (p. 2). Through professionalism, occupations organise their work, claiming legitimacy, public prestige and economic privilege in the marketplace. Put differently, professionalism is an institutional logic through which professions consolidate their identity and survive financially.

Human rights collectives have pursued professionalism to claim marketable visual expertise over the production, verification and use of various images of suffering. Through tailored video production, standards and training, they have sought to position their work vis-à-vis the needs of other institutional and legal milieux (Ristovska 2021). For example, human rights collectives curate eyewitness videos for reports intended to "look like news" so they are more likely to appear in mainstream news media (E. Daly, interview, 10 July 2019); they promote authentication standards that meet journalistic and legal requirements in various publications, such as the *Verification Handbook* (Silverman 2015) and the *Video as Evidence Field Guide* (WITNESS 2016); and they train activists, journalists, legal professionals and other actors in best practices for video documentation and usage deemed appropriate for specific decision-making contexts.

By mimicking other professional modalities and logics, the pursuit of professionalism has given rise to a so-called proxy profession, which does not have a professional independence, but it can better exist within and alongside the environments through which human rights claims receive fuller recognition and restitution (Ristovska 2021). As a qualifier, the term proxy draws from its literal meaning as substitute. By providing pragmatic solutions to various journalistic, legal and policy challenges with evidentiary standards and verification mechanisms for eyewitness video, human rights collectives put their visual expertise to work for other professions. At the same time, these collectives also end up standing in for broader publics – including the eyewitnesses and activists who record and upload videos on social media – in front of various institutional and legal stakeholders.

The development of the proxy profession has been discussed in greater detail in the context of human rights video activism (Ristovska 2021). Although video activism has traditionally existed as an occupational craft denoting a wide-ranging set of practices that voice critique against global violations of human dignity, two key developments have facilitated its shaping by the streams of professionalism. On the one hand, the incorporation of activist footage across journalistic, legal and political domains has created interconnected institutional circumstances that demand practices and doctrines that can account for new modes of visual evidence produced independent of the professional powers connected to institutions (Ristovska 2019). The concept of professionalism helps clarify how these circumstances have provided the interconnected institutional locus that supports the development and legitimation of the proxy profession (Ristovska 2021). On the other hand, different civil groups and social movements have turned into NGOs to secure better access to funding structures and decision-making processes, becoming key representatives of civic voices across institutions (Lang 2013). This so-called NGO-isation process has been vital to the global prominence of the human rights movement as well (Neier 2012), facilitating the institutional legitimacy of human rights collectives as information and advocacy actors who represent human rights voices. The NGO structure has also been critical for providing organisational home and economic support for the broader efforts to professionalise human rights video activism as a practice, thus sustaining the proxy profession.

The path towards professionalism unfolds at a critical time when eyewitness video is becoming a more central force that negotiates the interplay between various cultural and institutional mechanisms that ferret out human rights violations (Ristovska and Price, 2018). According to Pierre Bairin, former Multimedia Director at HRW, "video is not just an illustration on the side. It's really the material itself. It's part of the evidence, part of the story" (interview, New York City, 16 June 2015). For Priscila Neri, Associate Director at WITNESS, "video has the capacity to spark and catalyse processes for justice". As a result, human rights collectives now seek to "qualify the material from a strategic, substantive, and technical standpoint" so that it is more likely to be of use to news media, courts and various advocacy venues (interview, New York City, 6 August 2015). For example, WITNESS partnered with TRIAL International, an NGO supporting victims and fighting for impunity for international crimes, and eyeWitness to Atrocities, a human rights project founded by the International Bar Association, to conduct video-as-evidence training to assist lawyers in collecting and verifying eyewitness footage. The materials were then used as evidence of murder and torture constituting crimes against humanity in a case in front of the military tribunal in Bukavu, Democratic Republic of Congo in 2018 (Kumananga and Lumenje 2019).

In the context of social media specifically, the proxy professional status often puts human rights collectives in a better position to harness video's potential for justice and accountability than the activists and other eyewitnesses on the ground. Syrian Archive (2021), for example, assisted with the filling of a criminal complaint in France regarding chemical weapons attacks in August 2013 in Douma and Eastern Ghouta. Staffers stored and verified eyewitness videos from YouTube and other platforms that are now part of the documentary evidence for the criminal complaint filed in March 2021. In other words, the proxy profession is significant for the mediatisation of global wars and conflicts on social media because it brokers eyewitness videos in institutional and legal domains.

How the Proxy Profession Navigates the Social Media Landscape

Digital technologies and platforms have transformed the experiences of bearing witness to trauma into instantaneous media representations, shifting the focus away "from the existential struggle of the witness to the assessment of the authenticity, meaning, and significance of eyewitness images" (Mortensen 2015, 1398). Through the emerging legitimacy of the proxy profession, human rights collectives are becoming critical actors who sort through the avalanche of eyewitness images on social media, helping shape how wars and conflicts are represented and perceived across institutions. As a result, the proxy profession merits attention in its own right. In what follows, the chapter briefly maps how human rights collectives in their role as proxy professionals have been promoting evidentiary standards, investigative protocols and information policies for social media imagery to better play in different institutional and legal spaces. The proxy profession's policy orientation, however, also makes human rights collectives less able to resist various geopolitical and neoliberal frameworks that continue to undergird the mediated struggles for global human dignity.

Evidentiary Standards

In November 2014, a video, titled "SYRIAN HERO BOY rescue girl in shootout", was posted on the YouTube channel of Shaam Network, which is typically considered a reputable aggregator of Syrian eyewitness videos. News organisations like the BBC tried to confirm the authenticity of this viral video, concluding that it would be "very difficult to give a definitive opinion on whether it is fake or not" (BBC News 2014). Other news organisations quickly shared it as evidence of the horrors in Syria (e.g. Goldstein 2014). It turned out that the video was shot by a Norwegian director in Malta, mimicking the aesthetic qualities associated with eyewitness footage like shaky camera movements, to draw attention to the Syrian war. Meanwhile, WITNESS (2014) published a story on the verification challenges exemplified by this deceiving video, quoting one of its staffers:

> I keep a list of these types of videos to use when training human rights workers and journalists on video verification. Their eyes widen when they see that outlets ranging from the Washington Post and Al Arabiya to every TV news channel that has asked its audience to send in storm footage has been deceived by faked, manipulated, or recycled videos.
>
> *Para 7*

Such statements are not an isolated incident. Peter Bouckaert, a former Emergencies Division Director at HRW, claimed:

> I always chuckle when media talk about unverified videos because it's kind of a lazy shorthand because there are ways in which you can verify the information; there are ways in which you can even contact the very activist who uploaded the video to ask them more questions. It just takes doing your homework like with any other kind of reporting that you do.
>
> *Podcast, Holley, 2015*

These human rights collectives have sought to position their professionalisation endeavours as a response to the perceived deficiencies of mainstream news media

(Ristovska 2021). In this sense, pointing to news media's failure to properly authenticate eyewitness video is a discursive tactic that helps human rights collectives establish their own credibility and expertise around verification standards for visual evidence.

Standards are part of professionalism because they embody the ideals and principles that guide the development of specialised knowledge. Human rights collectives have worked to create and sustain evidentiary standards for eyewitness video as part of their broader efforts to professionalise video activism (Ristovska 2021). A defining moment is George Holliday's video of the beating of Rodney King by Los Angeles police officers in 1991, perhaps the most well-known case in the US that precipitated a shift in the role and scope of eyewitness video in journalism, the law and human rights practice. At the time, however, there was a scepticism in the journalistic community about the broader value of such footage. To give just one example, the Poynter Institute was worried that "It's hard enough for journalists to monitor the work of other journalists, but when you add to that the work of amateurs, the situation becomes impossible" (Cobb 1995). By contrast, WITNESS interpreted Holliday's tape as a game changer for human rights practice, using it as its founding story. In addition to distributing cameras and co-producing videos with other activists at the time, it also built the human rights channel The Hub as a repository of eyewitness videos, seeking to advocate "for a new global standard for human rights video online" (Thijm 2010).

Other human rights collectives followed suit. When Amnesty launched the Citizen Evidence Lab, an online platform dedicated to video verification training, skills and resources, the Poynter Institute enthusiastically proclaimed that "Amnesty International is in the verification game and that is good news for journalism" (Silverman 2014). The Citizen Evidence Lab includes guides on how to conduct effective online inquiries, tips for viewing and verifying online videos, case studies and other resources and tools for authenticating and archiving eyewitness footage. The prevailing assumption has been that human rights collectives can help not only activists but also journalists to develop skills to better evaluate and use eyewitness images in news reporting. This assumption provides context for the emerging cross-hiring trends in journalism and human rights practice, with former Amnesty, HRW and HRC staffers currently working for digital investigation teams at news organisations like the New York Times.

The law, like journalism, has also struggled establishing unified guidance and archival standards for eyewitness video (Feigenson and Spiesel 2009; Freeman and Llorente 2021; Ristovska 2020). Widely accepted evidentiary and archival standards for video evidence writ large either vary by legal jurisdictions or are simply non-existent. Human rights collectives like HRC, HRW, Syrian Archive and WITNESS have thus worked with the International Criminal Court (ICC), the United Nations Office of the High Commissioner for Human Rights (OHCHR), the International, Impartial and Independent Mechanism on international crimes committed in Syria, the Institute for War, Holocaust and Genocide Studies, and other institutions to standardise verification and archival mechanisms for eyewitness video in order to strengthen its evidentiary potential in international criminal investigations and trials. Furthermore, human rights staffers sit on the ICC's Technology Advisory Board that guides the court on new forms of digital evidence like eyewitness video from social media. They also elaborate on these standards in various publications, including those by academic presses (e.g. Dubberley et al. 2020; Gregory 2015).

To support the establishment of consistent standards, HRC and OHCHR published the *Berkeley Protocol on Digital Open Source Investigations* in 2020. The Berkeley Protocol follows two earlier UN initiatives: the Minnesota Protocol on the Investigation of Potentially Unlawful Death and the Manual on the Effective Investigation and Documentation of Torture and Other Cruel, Inhuman or Degrading Treatment or Punishment. The editorial and advisory committees included not only legal experts but also human rights staffers. The Berkeley Protocol provides international standards and guidance for human rights investigators, including media outlets, civil society groups, national and international agencies and courts.

The evidentiary standards are further promoted through training. In addition to human rights workers and journalists, these collectives train judges, attorneys, civil society groups and activists. According to Alexa Koenig, Executive Director at HRC, it is important to prepare "judges for the kinds of open-source information that human rights advocates around the world are increasingly collecting" (phone interview, 8 July 8 2019). For Kelly Matheson, Associate Director at WITNESS who leads the Video as Evidence Programme, "activists really need to know a little bit about the law, and lawyers need to know a little bit about filming so they can communicate with each other" (interview, New York City, 22 July 2015). Training is intended to teach activists how reliability and relevance are established and how crimes are proved in court as well as to help judges and attorneys learn how to probe and ask pertinent questions about the video materials submitted as evidence. In other words, human right collectives promote evidentiary standards for eyewitness video through different publications and training programmes for relevant stakeholders.

Investigative Protocols

As triangulation between eyewitness media, satellite imagery and on-the-ground research has become the gold standard in human rights fact-finding (C. Koettl, interview, Washington DC, 20 July 2015), human rights collectives further implement and promote these evidentiary standards in their investigative work. Amnesty, HRW, HRC and Syrian Archive have established teams and units dedicated to digital investigations that rely on eyewitness video, satellite imagery and other online information. Amnesty even runs two specialised programmes: the Decoder Project, an online platform that sends out verification tasks to hundreds of volunteers from around the world, and Digital Verification Corps Programme, a partnership with seven universities in the US, Canada, Mexico, UK, South Africa and Hong Kong, that trains students on how to verify eyewitness imagery and then uses the students' work to support the reporting by Amnesty's research teams. For example, the Decoder Project relied on 7,280 volunteers to map surveillance cameras in New York City and to advocate for a citywide ban on facial recognition technology (Decode Surveillance NYC 2021). The Digital Verification Corps at Cambridge University and University of Pretoria preserved and verified eyewitness imagery from the November 2019 protests in Iran, documenting the deaths of 304 men, women and children killed by Iran's security forces (Rogers et al. 2020).

The investigative protocols and methodologies also address journalistic and legal needs, leading to collaborative work. There are many examples: HRC's Investigations Lab worked with the Associated Press to uncover how Myanmar security forces used bodies as tools of terror by verifying 2,000 tweets and eyewitness videos (McDowell and Mason 2021); HRC also conducted research for the Washington Post investigation into an unjustified arrest of four Black Lives Matter protestors in Portland ("Video Shows Federal Agents", 2020); and Amnesty collaborated with BBC Africa and others on the Peabody-winning investigation, *Anatomy of a Killing*, about state violence in Cameroon (BBC News 2018). Syrian Archive has filed criminal complaints against Syrian officials not only in France but also in Germany (Moody 2020). Amnesty obtained and verified eyewitness video used in a Stockholm District Court case involving a rebel fighter in Syria (Aksamitowska 2021). The proxy profession's legitimacy creates these opportunities for human rights collectives to collaborate with established news organisations and to contribute to the evidentiary display of court cases. In doing so, the proxy profession helps leverage eyewitness video's evidentiary, policy and advocacy potential in achieving human rights goals, increasing the likelihood that such footage does not get lost in the social media streams but becomes part of public, institutional and legal debates.

Information Policy

The proxy profession also enables human rights collectives to be involved with information policy making, especially around social media content removal. This issue became prominent when Facebook removed an eyewitness video in 2017 that was part of the evidentiary basis for the ICC's arrest warrant for an alleged commander in Libya accused of having committed or ordered 33 murders in Benghazi (e.g. Al Jaloud et al. 2019). Facebook argued that the graphic footage violated the platform's terms-of-service agreement by promoting terrorist propaganda even though the video was valuable as legal evidence. Removals like this one have become a rather common practice among social media companies, and governments around the world have encouraged this trend (Human Rights Watch 2020). According to Dia Kayyali, former Programme Manager for Tech + Advocacy at WITNESS and currently at Mnemonic, "the big concern that we have is that human rights content is getting deleted at an astonishing rate, especially with this hyper focus on removing so-called extremist content" (WhatsApp interview, 16 July 2019). Defining extremist content and terrorist propaganda is subject to political contestation in its own right as exemplified by Facebook's censorship of Kurdish politicians in Turkey (Tufekci 2017). In the push for social media content regulation with respect to extremism and propaganda, potentially important evidentiary materials for human rights work are also disappearing, but the public has little insight into the corporate decision making and the black-box algorithms involved.

The deletion problem increased during the Covid-19 pandemic. Content moderators work as contractors, not full-time employees, so they were placed on leave. Social media companies claimed that content moderation is a sensitive work that cannot be done remotely, so they deployed more artificial intelligence technologies, reducing users' ability to appeal removal decisions. In May 2020 alone, Syrian Archive discovered that more than 350,000 videos had disappeared from YouTube, including videos of aerial attacks, protests and destruction of civilian homes in Syria. The rate of content takedowns at YouTube increased by 20% from the previous year (Asher-Schapiro and Barkawi 2020).

Human rights collectives have been able to appeal some of these decisions and subsequently restore eyewitness videos along with activist and local news media accounts. Yet social media companies have also refused to re-post or to share the removed content with these human rights collectives (Human Rights Watch 2020). Some eyewitness videos are also deleted by algorithms at the time of upload with no public record of their existence. National law enforcement officials can use warrants, subpoenas and court orders to compel social media companies to hand over known removed content, but international investigators lack such legal power. Gambia therefore had to go through the US District Court for the District of Columbia to get Facebook to release Myanmar officials' data for a genocide case submitted to the International Court of Justice (Robertson 2021).

To address this problem with content moderation, human rights collectives have started advocating for policy changes and best practices that preserve online imagery and data that may be valuable as human rights evidence. Dia Kayyali, for example, testified in front of the European Union Parliament on social media content removal in March 2019. HRW (2020) has recommended following the model for child sexual exploitation online. In the US, social media platforms are legally required to take down such content and then to share a copy and relevant metadata with the National Center for Missing and Exploited Children, which has a legal right to possess such materials indefinitely and to co-operate with law enforcement nationally and internationally. HRC (2021) has developed a typology of archives with four models that could be used to preserve online human rights content with overview of legal obligations, challenges and end-uses. By proposing policies for social media content regulation, human rights collectives are further solidifying their professional expertise. Through the proxy profession, they can represent human rights activist and public concerns across policy-relevant contexts, shaping which eyewitness videos have the potential to be seen online and to be further used in institutional and legal decision making.

As eyewitness video competes for visibility and legitimacy via the various technological, cultural, legal and political dynamics that characterise today's social media landscape, the proxy profession empowers human rights collectives to better navigate these spaces. The evidentiary standards, investigative protocols and information policies put forward by these collectives can broaden the reach of eyewitness videos across human rights-related contexts. This achievement is indeed significant, making sure that the efforts of eyewitnesses who record and post videos on social media are not completely void and have the potential to trigger processes for justice and accountability. Yet as Eliot Freidson (2001) argues, professionalism is a logic that can be susceptible to market demands for profit and efficiency. Furthermore, human rights work has long operated in a highly politicised terrain, so no eyewitness video, irrespective of its authenticity, can be a neutral tool for human rights and social change. The chapter thus concludes with a discussion about the proxy profession's vulnerability to neoliberal and geopolitical paradigms that can shape which human rights claims receive recognition, how, and why.

How the Proxy Profession Responds to Broader Challenges to Human Dignity

Eyewitness videos that provide a glimpse into possible human rights violations are powerful, public moments of testimony that inevitably provoke intense struggles over the right to their meaning. They often epitomise what Lilie Chouliaraki and Mette Mortensen (2022) call "flesh witnessing", video testimonies recorded under circumstances of life and death that shed light on violence, trauma and injustice. As such, eyewitness videos make ethical and political appeals. Through the act of recording and uploading the footage on social media, their producers assert themselves as political actors: they seek a change in status from mere witnesses (or victims) of violence to active conflict participants who claim their fundamental human right to communicate. Turning these video materials into court evidence, using them in a human rights investigation and preserving their otherwise ephemeral existence on social media can be important efforts in the global fight for human rights.

By aspiring to professionalism, human rights collectives like Amnesty, HRW, HRC, Syrian Archive and WITNESS secure access – however weak or strong – to decision-making settings. They can therefore shape eyewitness video strategically as a policy-oriented mechanism for change (e.g. using the footage as legal evidence, as forensic record or as medium and content for policy debate). In the process, these human rights collectives are becoming better positioned to legitimise online video's testimonial capacity to produce institutionally and legally meaningful human rights claims than the various eyewitnesses on the ground who risk their own lives to produce and upload the footage. As a result, the proxy profession embraces a representative function which, despite its pragmatic policy achievements, is not immune to the long-standing neoliberal and geopolitical dynamics characterising the human rights field. The need to maintain institutional and professional legitimacy to enter the spaces where broader human rights agendas get developed as well as the competition for funding and responsibility towards donors to secure financial survival all motivate the proxy profession to prioritise measurable short-term goals over long-term structural changes (Ristovska 2021). It is not surprising, then, that Amnesty and HRW, for example, have utilised eyewitness videos to produce numerous investigations into Israel's violation of international laws of war without necessarily questioning the state of war itself.

Though 9/11 crystalised the political shift away from opposing the crime of war to opposing war crimes, Samuel Moyn (2021) traces this Western embrace of a so-called humane war back to the 19th century when the founders of the Red Cross saw war as unavoidable and merely advocated for making it less lethal. As part of the larger social, political and legal processes to normalise such wars, the claims, the stories and voices of those who produce and upload eyewitness videos on social media directly from the scenes of trauma and violence often get lost or caught up in the global hierarchies of human life and the political economy surrounding the production and use of evidence (e.g. Andén-Papadopoulos 2020; Della Ratta 2018; Ginsburg 2021). Put differently, the proxy profession exposes injustice by rescuing the institutional and legal powers that tolerate, and indeed justify, certain violations of human dignity. The proxy profession is thus limited in its ability to facilitate alternative spaces where moral and political communities come together to propose bold programmes for human rights and social change.

As eyewitness video provides a critical mode for accessing global wars and conflicts, the proxy profession will continue to play a pivotal role in how and to what ends these materials are used across institutional and legal domains. Viewing human rights collectives as proxy professionals and mapping their work is therefore an important task for thinking about the power and limitation of social media images to facilitate justice and to protect human rights.

Note

1 This chapter draws from and expands upon research conducted for my book *Seeing Human Rights: Video Activism as a Proxy Profession* (MIT Press, 2021). For a more detailed methodological discussion, please see Ristovska, 2021, 18–19.

Bibliography

Aksamitowska, K. 2021. "Digital evidence in domestic core international crimes prosecutions: Lessons learned from Germany, Sweden, Finland, and The Netherlands. *Journal of International Criminal Justice* 19, no. 1: 189–211.

Al Jaloud, A. R., H. Al Khatib, J. Deutch, D. Kayyali, and J. C. York. 2019. "Caught in the net: The impact of 'extremist' speech regulations on human rights content." *Electronic Frontier Foundation*, May 2009. Retrieved from: www.eff.org/files/2019/05/30/caught_in_the_net_whitepaper_2019.pdf

Allan, S. 2013. *Citizen witnessing: Revisioning journalism in times of crisis.* Cambridge: Polity Press.

Andén-Papadopoulos, K. 2020. "The 'image-as-forensic-evidence' economy in the post-2011 Syrian conflict: The power and constraints of contemporary practices of video activism." *International Journal of Communication* 14: 5072–5091.

Asher-Schapiro, A. and B. Barkawi. 2020. "'Lost memories:' War crimes evidence threatened by AI moderation. *Reuters*, June 19. Retrieved from: www.reuters.com/article/us-glo bal-socialmedia-rights-trfn/lost-memories-war-crimes-evidence-threatened-by-ai-mod eration-idUSKBN23Q2TO

Askanius, T. 2020. "Video activism as technology, text, testimony—or practices." In *Citizen media and practice: Currents, connections, challenge*, edited by H. C. Stephansen and E. Treré, 136–151. Oxon: Routledge.

BBC News. 2014. "#BBCtrending: Is video of Syrian 'Hero Boy' authentic?" *BBC*, November 14. Retrieved from: www.bbc.com/news/av/magazine-30043574

BBC News. 2018. *Anatomy of a killing. BBC*, September 24. Retrieved from: www.youtube.com/watch?v=4G9S-eoLgX4

Chouliaraki, L. and M. Mortensen. 2022. "Flesh Witnessing: Smartphones, UGC and Embodied Testimony." *Journalism* 23, no 3: 591-598.

Cobb, C. 1995. "Amateur videotapes changing perspective of news." *Gazette*, February 26.

Decode Surveillance NYC. 2021. *Amnesty International*. Retrieved from: https://decoders.amnesty.org/projects/decode-surveillance

Della Ratta, D. 2018. *Shooting a revolution: Visual media and warfare in Syria.* London: Pluto Press.

Dubberley, S., A. Koenig, and D. Murray, eds. 2020. *Digital witness: Using open source information for human rights investigation, documentation and accountability*. New York: Oxford University Press.

Elliott, P. 1972. *The sociology of professions*. London: Macmillan.

Feigenson, N. and C. Spiesel. 2009. *Law on display: The digital transformation of legal persuasion and judgment*. New York: New York University Press.

Freeman, L. and R.V. Llorente. 2021. "Finding the signal in the noise: International criminal evidence and procedure in the digital age." *Journal of International Criminal Justice* 19, no. 1: 163–188.

Freidson, E. 2001. *Professionalism, the third logic: On the practices of knowledge*. Chicago: University of Chicago Press.

Ginsburg, R. 2021. "Emancipation and collaboration: A critical examination of human rights video advocacy." *Theory, Culture & Society* 38, no. 3: 51–70.

Goldstein, S. 2014. "WATCH: Syrian Boy Hero braves sniper fire to save tiny girl trapped by barrage of bullets." *NY Daily News*, November 11. Retrieved from: www.nydailynews.com/news/world/syrian-boy-hero-braves-sniper-fire-save-tiny-girl-article-1.2006869

Gregory, S. 2015. "Ubiquitous witnesses: Who creates the evidence and the live(d) experience of human rights violations?" *Information, Communication, & Society* 18, no. 11: 1378–1392.

Holley, A. 2015. *HRWFF podcast with Peter Bouckaert*. Human Rights Watch Film Festival Podcast. MP3 audio, 23:37.

Human Rights Center. 2021. "Digital lockers: Archiving social media evidence of atrocity crimes." Retrieved from: https://humanrights.berkeley.edu/sites/default/files/digi tal_lockers_report5.pdf

Human Rights Center and United Nations Office of the High Commissioner for Human Rights. 2020. "Berkeley Protocol on Digital Open Source Investigation: A practical guide on the effective use of digital open source information in investigating violations of international criminal, human rights and humanitarian law." Retrieved from: www.ohchr.org/Documents/Publications/OHCHR_BerkeleyProtocol.pdf

Human Rights Watch. 2020. "'Video unavailable:' Social media platforms remove evidence of war crimes." *Human Rights Watch*, September 10. Retrieved from: www.hrw.org/rep ort/2020/09/10/video-unavailable/social-media-platforms-remove-evidence-war-cri mes#_ftn36

Kumananga and Lumenje. 2019. "Two Congolese villages gone from tragedy to hope." *Trial International*, May 3. Retrieved from: https://trialinternational.org/latest-post/kamana nga-and-lumenje-two-congolese-villages-gone-from-tragedy-to-hope/

Lang, S. 2013. *NGOs, civil society, and the public sphere*. New York: Cambridge University Press.

Larson, M. S. 1977. *The rise of professionalism: A sociological analysis*: Berkeley: University of California Press.

McDowell, R. and M. Mason. 2021. "AP investigation: Myanmar's Junta using bodies to terrorize." *AP News*, May 26. Retrieved from: https://apnews.com/article/myanmar-business-b2187c696e428139437778aeab0c43d4

McPherson, E. 2016. "Source credibility as 'Information Subsidy:' Strategies for successful NGO journalism at Mexican Human Rights NGOs." *Journal of Human Rights* 15, no. 3: 330–346.

Moody, O. 2020. "Assad Trials brace Germany for new Nuremberg." *The Times*, December 25. Retrieved from: www.thetimes.co.uk/article/assad-trials-brace-germany-for-new-nuremberg-gr5bvtmld

Mortensen, M. 2015. "Connective witnessing: Reconfiguring the relationship between the individual and the collective." *Information, Communication & Society* 18, no. 11: 1393–1406.

Moyn, S. 2021. *Humane: How the United States abandoned peace and reinvented war*. New York: Parrar, Straus and Giroux.

Neier, A. 2012. *International human rights movement: A history*. Princeton: Princeton University Press.

Ristovska, S. 2019. "Human rights collectives as visual experts: The case of Syrian archive." *Visual Communication* 18, no. 3: 333–351.

Ristovska, S. 2020. "The need for visual information policy." *Surveillance & Society* 18, no. 3: 418–421.

Ristovska, S. 2021. *Seeing human rights: Video activism as a proxy profession*. Cambridge: MIT Press.

Ristovska, S. and M. Price, eds. 2018. *Visual imagery and human rights practice*. New York: Palgrave.

Robertson, A. 2021. "Judge orders Facebook to hand over Myanmar officials' hate posts for genocide case." *The Verge*, September 23. Retrieved from: www.theverge.com/2021/9/23/22689559/facebook-rohingya-myanmar-official-data-order-gambia-genocide-trial

Rogers, D., R. A. R Farr, M. Mahmoudi, and M. Dastbaz. 2020. "How Amnesty's Digital Verification Corps documented the November 2019 protests in Iran. *Citizen Evidence Lab*, December 7. Retrieved from: https://citizenevidence.org/2020/12/07/cambri dge-dvc-iran/

Silverman, C. 2014. "Amnesty International launches video verification tool." *Poynter Institute*, July 8. Retrieved from: www.poynter.org/reporting-editing/2014/amnesty-internatio nal-launches-video-verification-tool-website/

Silverman, C., ed. 2015. V*erification handbook for investigative reporting: A guide to online search and research techniques for using UGC and open source information in investigations*. Maastricht: European Journalism Centre. Retrieve from http://verificationhandbook. com/book2/

Syrian Archive. 2021. "Survivors and the Syrian Center for Media and Freedom of Expression, with support from Syrian Archive and the Justice Initiative, seek French Criminal Investigations of Chemical Attacks in the city of Douma in Syria [Press Release]." *Syrian Archive*, March 2. Retrieved from https://syrianarchive.org/en/investigations/Frenchcr iminalinvestigation

Thijm, Y. A. 2010. "Update on The Hub and WITNESS' New Online Strategy." *WITNESS Blog*, August. Retrieved from: https://blog.witness.org/2010/08/update-on-the-hub-and-witness-new-online-strategy/

Thorsen, E. & S. Allan, eds. 2014. *Citizen journalism: Global perspectives. Vol. 2*. New York: Peter Lang Publishing.

Tufekci, Z. 2017. *Twitter and tear gas: The power and fragility of networked protest*. New Haven: Yale University Press.

Video Shows Federal Agents Detained People in Portland Based on Inaccurate, Insufficient Information. 2020. *Washington Post*, September 10. Retrieved from: www.youtube.com/watch?v=EkISH8jKFsE

Weizman, E. 2017. *Forensic architecture: Violence at the threshold of detectability*. Brooklyn: Zone Books.

WITNESS. 2014. "Will the Syrian Hero Boy make us question everything we see? (And why don't we do that already?). *WITNESS Media Lab*, November 2014. Retrieved from: https://lab.witness.org/syrian-hero-boy/

WITNESS. 2016. "Video as evidence field guide." *WITNESS*. Retrieved from: https://vae.witness.org/video-as-evidence-field-guide/

3

INCENDIARY IMAGES

Visual Reportage of Syria's Civil War

Stuart Allan

Syria's ongoing civil war has been widely characterised as the most collectively mediated conflict in history, such is the scopic diversity of contrasting forms of journalistic relay produced, brokered, curated and shared across digital news networks and social media platforms. While exultant declarations heralding YouTube, Facebook or Twitter "revolutions" have unravelled, there is little doubt that what is believed to be true about the conflict, particularly for those without direct experience of its terrors, continues to be decisively shaped by the evidentiary images and counter-images of visual reportage.

From the outset of the national crisis in 2011, the Bashar al-Assad regime's attempts to control the field of vision – and thereby constrain global media narratives – entailed invoking severe measures to curtail the number of foreign correspondents on the ground. International news organisations were acutely aware the procuration of imagery would not be centralised in the hands of professional photojournalists and videographers. Many were already reliant upon local journalists for visual reportage, as well as ordinary Syrians prepared to risk their safety to craft personal forms of citizen witnessing. This institutional dependency on burgeoning participatory cultures, including engagements with fast-coalescing diasporic communities across social media, seemed remarkable to observers at the time (Al-Ghazzi 2014; Harkin et al. 2012; Howard and Hussain 2013; RWB 2013; Trombetta 2012). Variously labelled as "citizen journalism", "user-generated content" (UGC) or "amateur photojournalism", amongst alternative terms, such reportage supplemented – indeed, in some instances, supplanted – professional news coverage from afflicted areas. Its use-value for media outlets involved collaborative negotiation, being contingent upon due verification and curation, with considerable effort expended to confirm authenticity through editorial protocols. Such validity checks were challenging to administer at the best of times, let alone under pressure in a profoundly volatile crisis, but the evidence gathered proved vital for

DOI: 10.4324/9781003176923-4

purposes of accuracy while, at the same time, counteracting propaganda and disinformation disseminated by the regime.

This chapter addresses this volume's overarching themes by examining professional and citizen-led visual reportage of the Syrian catastrophe from March 2011 onwards, paying particular attention to social media contexts. At the time of writing, the deaths of almost 500,000 people have been registered by the Syrian Observatory for Human Rights (2021), with tens of thousands of others missing and presumed dead. Included in these calculations are an estimated 159,774 civilians killed so far, many of whom believed to have been tortured to death in detention centres (SOHR 2021). In pinpointing several formative developments consolidating over this period, this chapter assesses the relative affordances and limitations associated with a variety of initiatives – inclusive of news organisations' networking of visible evidence gathering, to vernacular forms of folk image-making, to activist film collectives such as Abounaddara – intended to document the daily horrors of violence. Delving beneath broad assertions regarding the apparent "democratisation" of digital war coverage, it tracks the provenance of still and video imagery produced from places otherwise inaccessible to Western camera lenses. In the course of evaluating such initiatives, this chapter endeavours to contribute to wider debates regarding the visualisation of war and conflict, showing how an analysis of the lived materialities of reportage opens up fresh opportunities for critical understandings of alternate forms, practices and epistemes of truth-seeking.

Targeting Truth

Recognising the ten-year anniversary of the "Arab Spring" civic uprisings in 2021, Western media commentaries typically offered evaluative assessments of relative achievements and setbacks from one national context to the next in the region. Tunisia's fragile yet resilient democratic reforms were frequently described as exceptions to the revolutionary failures continuing to unfold elsewhere. In the words of a *Guardian* (2021) editorial leader observing the anniversary, "a decade after the region rose up against its dictators, authoritarianism has a tighter grip than ever, and its people are drained or traumatised". The blame, it continued, "does not rest with those who sought freedom, but the rulers who chose to crush them and the foreign powers whose interference has deepened and worsened the region's devastation" (Guardian 2021). Insurgencies demanding new rights and freedoms from oppressive regimes sparked state repression and crackdowns of a lethal ferocity that few were expecting in the initial euphoria, unleashing chaotic instability and, in the case of Syria, a civil war with no clear end in sight.

Violence erupted in Syria's southwestern city of Daraa in March 2011, first when 15 young boys accused of painting revolutionary graffiti were arrested and tortured, and then on the 18th of that month when security forces opened fire on a pro-democracy demonstration calling for an end to corruption and release of the children, taking the lives of several protestors (HRW 2011). As the rapid escalation of the crisis began to focus global attention, the authorities imposed an information blockade in a desperate effort to quell dissent by silencing the regime's enraged critics. A Human Rights Watch (HRW) report released in June accused the country's security forces of systematic killings and torture, while also pointing out how the Daraa blackout was intended to ensure these crimes were not exposed. As it stated:

> No independent observers could enter the city and one international jour-
> nalist who managed to report from Daraa during the first two weeks of
> protests in March was arrested upon his return to Damascus. During the
> siege all means of communication were shut down, including Syrian cell
> phone networks. Many witnesses told Human Rights Watch that cell phones
> were the first thing authorities confiscated during searches in their houses
> or at checkpoints. They were specifically looking for footage of the events
> and arrested and tortured those whom they suspected of trying to send out
> images or other information out, including some foreign nationals.
>
> *HRW 2011, 5–6*

Western correspondents – increasingly being blamed as "instigators" in state-controlled media coverage – struggled to make the most of relatively unfettered access while it lasted. For photojournalists seasoned by hard-won experience in the field, the influx of young (many under 30 years of age), unproven photographers joining them was concerning, if not alarming. Many of those intent on landing their first assignment in a war zone were self-financing, arriving without combat training, or even basic equipment such as helmets, flak jackets or medical kits. Some lacked professional camera gear, not knowing how to avoid its confiscation by airport security, or insisted they preferred to travel light with portable cameras or mobile telephones. "To me and some of the older crowd", Michael Kamber (2011) maintained, "there was a nagging suspicion that these packs of 'green' photographers were not taking war seriously – that they were joyriding, with all the casual priv- ilege the term implies". Still, he conceded, as unprepared as many of them were to cope with the dangers, "everyone – even a conflict photographer – has to start somewhere".

The perils for journalists and media workers became front-page news the world over on 22 February 2012, following the deliberate targeting of a makeshift media centre by President al-Assad's security forces in Baba Amr, a suburban neighbour- hood of Homs. Much of the ensuing media attention revolved around Marie Colvin, an eminent war correspondent for *The Sunday Times* (London), killed when a rocket hit the house in which she and other journalists had taken refuge during an onslaught of shelling. French photojournalist Rémi Ochlik died alongside Colvin that day. Time and again, references to the importance of bearing witness were highlighted in press accounts, Ochlik's name being added to a lengthening list of photojournalists killed or wounded in service to their craft and its publics. "His being there allowed the world to witness horrifying atrocities", Nate Rawlings (2012) of *Time* commented, "but it ended the life of a gifted storyteller when his own adventure had barely begun". Amongst those surviving the carnage were freelance photographer Paul Conroy along with Edith Bouvier, a French correspondent for *Le Figaro*, both of whom suffered serious injuries. At risk of bleeding to death, they were treated in a house turned clinic nearby. A retired surgeon tended to their wounds, improvising with what was at hand (iodine, a toothbrush and an office stapler) for medical equipment. Several bids to rescue the two failed before they were finally smuggled out of Homs by activists.

As the al-Assad regime struggled to police its preferred narratives in the ensuing furore of international condemnation, namely that the protestors were radical Islamist terrorists colluding with nefarious outsiders to destroy the country, further restrictions were imposed on news organisations' access. Several Western editors complied with demands to leave the country, already aware they were unable to ensure adequate safety measures for their colleagues in the field. Meanwhile the national and local media were subjected to ever greater pressure to uphold a pro-Assad line, reportage blurring into disinformation, propaganda and, with growing frequency, conspiratorial projections of enmity (Linfield 2019; Tepperman 2015). For those journalists engaged in daringly defiant reporting, longstanding censorship restrictions prohibiting criticism of the regime were severely enforced, with perceived transgressors of officially sanctioned boundaries swiftly punished (HRW 2015; Taub 2016). The "iron-fisted tactics" of the Syrian authorities, Salama (2012) contended, meant reporters "were further strangulated, and many went missing, one after the other, with no hint of their whereabouts" (2012: 517). With state power in the balance, she added, "it was clear that the Syrian regime would not show mercy to journalists, native or foreign" (2012, 517; see also Cottle et al. 2016).

Under these circumstances, countless protestors, activists, lawyers, medical personnel, fieldworkers, community volunteers, accidental bystanders and the like felt compelled to step up their efforts to generate vernacular forms of folk image-making and self-documentation to forge communities of protest across social media. "An entire army of citizen journalists, armed with cellular phones, video cameras, Skype, and the all-important Internet connection, are ensuring that the events unfolding in Homs are made accessible, often in real-time, to a global viewership", Heras (2012) wrote at the time. "Through their actions, these Syrian citizen journalists are shaping the international perception of their revolution in a gritty, uncensored manner". Intent on waging battle over public opinion, many acquired new image-making skills in order to assemble visual evidence of atrocities and human rights abuses the world – they assumed – would not ignore. For others, being a first-person narrator, perhaps in the impromptu role of a video-activist, meant they were able to reaffirm a sense of agency by articulating their opposition to the regime. With Western editors and journalists becoming reliant upon them for on the ground perspectives, however, the corresponding duty of care became evermore pronounced. "The Syrian security agencies are making unprecedented efforts to identify those who help foreign reporters", Reporters Without Borders (RWB) warned in November 2011, placing them and their families in danger of severe reprisals (RWB 2011). Despite these perilous conditions, verified eyewitness "amateur" still and video footage were widely recognised for narrowing the media gap, including by the RWB with its 2012 Netizen Prize awarded to Syrian citizen journalists and human rights activists. "Netizens are more and more persecuted", namely "because they have become instrumental in the news gathering process", RWB president Dominique Gerbaud stated, pointing to the government's "increasingly sophisticated methods of censorship, surveillance and repression" (cited in RWB 2012).

A tragic case in point was former vegetable seller turned citizen journalist, Ali Mahmoud Othman, credited with being one of the first to video the unrest in Homs. He played a crucial role in the media centre assisting foreign correspondents, including in the evacuation to save the lives of Conroy and Bouvier after the centre's bombardment. Arrested by a military intelligence unit shortly afterwards in Aleppo on 28 March, it was soon feared Othman was being subjected to severe torture after being transferred to a Damascus prison. "If it wasn't for him, no Western media would have been able to work in Baba Amr and bear witness to the slaughter of the civilian population", Conroy told CNN when calling for Othman's immediate release from detention (cited in CNN 2012). Known as "The Eyes of Baba Amr", Othman earned the admiration of those around him for courageous reporting. "He had no background in journalism and learnt by watching others", Monica Prieto, a Spanish journalist, told the *Sunday Times*. "On the last day in Homs when everybody left, he stayed. He said that if there are people who cannot leave, I have to stay", she added. "So he stayed in Homs during the invasion at great risk and continued to document events" (cited in Macleod and Flamand 2012). Despite international appeals for his freedom from custody, Othman died in prison on 30 December 2013 (CPJ 2013; RWB 2019). No cause of death was revealed, the regime's brutal message to activists and citizen journalists' intent on truth-seeking being perfectly clear.

Digital Visibilities

"Networked images are performative, in that they gain value (therefore 'meaning') through circulation and shareability", Della Ratta (2021) observes, "determined not only by human interaction as measured by how many people like, share, retweet, and repost them, but also by virtue of the technological infrastructure supporting these very interactions (the interface, the database, the algorithm)" (2021, 72). The valiant commitment shown by so many Syrian citizens to produce visual documentation using their mobile cell phones or video cameras – swiftly uploading what was often raw, visceral imagery and footage via social media platforms, blogs, live stream sites and the like – enhanced foreign journalists' efforts to focus the attention economy of global news organisations. Inspired by a host of varied motivations, this civic reportage made possible fresh insight into breaking developments, often with unsettling immediacy. To be caught producing such material would almost certainly mean imprisonment, or worse, yet they persisted, best they were able, in the near-absence of trained professionals. For some, the decision to bear witness was a spontaneous one, while for others, it has been thought through beforehand, a more self-reflexively informed sense of journalism underwriting their work. In repurposing networks to capture and narrativise the "real truth" of warfare in all of its horror, some recognised a mutual investment in legitimacy between citizen practitioners and international news organisations (whether the latter be al-Jazeera and al-Arabiya or Western counterparts), each looking to the other for validation. In any case, diaspora activists worked to smuggle digital cameras and equipment for them into the country, while also helping to improve the distribution of their embodied forms of eyewitnessing across ad hoc participatory cultures circumventing Assad's media blackout (Della Ratta 2018; Elias 2017; Johnston 2017). Low-resolution, pixelated images or jarring video footage seemed all the more authentic to many distant viewers, just as visuals considered too slick or polished risked seeming contrived or manipulated.

Without the benefit of formal training, several citizens adopting the role of photojournalist described how they taught themselves to create and compose images in a manner consistent with their understanding of war photography and its traditions. "I started following the photo pages of AFP, Reuters, *New York Times* and *Washington Post*", one such photographer explained when interviewed in Aleppo. "I would look at the photos from earlier wars to be able to form an idea of the photo. And little by little, I started getting experience with photography" (cited in Mollerup and Mortensen 2020, 737). Such efforts to amplify voices necessitated honing new skills to achieve the expected standard of professional quality, as well as learning to see differently, including with respect to aesthetic sensibilities, so as to better predict and thereby produce the type of image likely to gain wider dissemination. Forging relationships with distribution networks – here Western NGOs often providing vital support in addition to that afforded by news organisations – required careful negotiation, even with so many photographers waiving financial compensation for putting their lives at risk. "My goal is to stop the bombardments", another citizen photographer explained, "and this is done by making sure it reaches the general public and they see what is happening to our children" (cited in Mollerup and Mortensen 2020, 741). Further logistical factors have included alliances with armed groups for access and protection, similarly raising ethical concerns for the photographers' lived precarity. Being citizens of Aleppo, these photographers have been immersed in the conflict, Mollerup and Mortensen (2020) point out, yet the lack of clarity in their status vis-à-vis news organisations – "as sources, freelancers, activists, citizen media actors, and so on" – has effectively "disqualified them from obtaining the safety, recognition and financial rewards granted to acknowledged journalists" (2020, 742).

Criticisms of citizen journalism's reportorial integrity, often revolving around arguments that it cannot be trusted until properly corroborated, were waning as the war wore on. This was principally due to growing perceptions that the gap between "amateur" and "professional" video and photo-reportage was narrowing. Characteristics commonly attributed to the former – precipitous, impressionistic and overly-subjective treatments, hampered by shaky camerawork and grainy focus, ill-considered aesthetics, or questionable news quality and framing – were increasingly being recalibrated and refined as citizen expertise developed. Proficiency in emulating production values and presentational standards markedly improved prospects for inclusion in international news coverage. Similarly, formal measures to reaffirm visual immediacy and transparency (at their most rudimentary, holding a daily newspaper in front of the lens at a readily identifiable place) were likewise regularised in adjudications of newsworthiness. Mistakes and misinterpretations happened, of course. Compromising gaps, oversights and errors were made by some citizens, notwithstanding their laudable intentions, while others have been exposed (albeit much less frequently than some critics have alleged) for deliberately misrepresenting, even inventing incidents so as to advance a particular strategic position or ideological claim. More typically, familiar criticisms of major media outlets – allegations they are inaccurate, unfair or stereotypical in their coverage – have been extended to citizen contributions as well. All too often, in aspiring to conform to prevailing Western news conventions, opportunities to enrich reportorial nuance, cultural specificity or rigour have been lost or diminished. Even worse, failing to complicate or disrupt these routine judgements has meant citizens' safety being placed at considerable risk, such as in the insistent demand for spectacular imagery for its shock value.

Partly in response to these types of concerns, several collaborative initiatives have emerged with the aim of recasting the fraught relationship between international news organisations, desperate for a competitive edge under intense pressures, and ordinary Syrians prepared to engage in news-making. The overriding interest of these news organisations, it has seemed to many video-activists and filmmakers, is to secure dramatic (at times voyeuristic, some believed) images quickly and cheaply from social media sites (Lynch et al. 2014; Mast and Hanegreefs 2015; Wardle et al. 2014; Wall and el Zahed 2015). Editorial and curatorial mediations recurrently reaffirm top-down calibrations of newsworthiness, with priority being awarded to visual tropes perceived to uphold institutionally ratified ways of seeing. At issue, it follows, has been a pressing need to reverse the logic whereby anonymous individuals continue to be effectively subcontracted to perform the labour of absent journalists and photojournalists.

This journalistic calculus has been difficult to rework, not least because it helps to deflect criticisms of ethical boundaries being crossed. "It gives television permission to exhibit bodies that have been murdered or humiliated on the simple pretext that it is Syrians themselves who create these images", Charif Kiwan (2014) of the anonymous film-making collective Abounaddara states bluntly. "In this way, the decline in the number of foreign correspondents in Syria who would be accountable for their work allows any potential blame for inappropriate images to be placed on the anonymous local source posting clips on YouTube". Founded in Damascus, Abounaddara ("the man with the glasses" in Arabic) is made up of self-taught, mostly women volunteers, who together have produced one short film every Friday since the earliest days of the insurgency. "Our notion of emergency was based on disturbing and inventing", its spokesperson Kiwan explains, "disturbing the machine that maintains the rules of the emergency situation, especially the rules of the film and media industries, and inventing new rules of representation" (interview with Bayoumi 2015). To overturn these "rules" entails advancing "the right to the image" as a new ethic of responsibility, that is, to empower fellow Syrians to produce their own images, respecting the principle of human dignity, independently from state control or media agendas. "Our spirit of filmmaking has always been to go for the countershot", Kiwan argues, "not to go where the mainstream media typically go, but to film the things happening elsewhere". Relayed via the internet, these documentary "bullet films" (most one or two minutes in length) "let images speak" without a voiceover, typically inscribing an aesthetic resistant to polarising us *versus* them binaries. Contradictory truths can be unsettling, making for uncomfortable viewing, while also affording insights into quotidian experiences of suffering and resilience. In challenging how "images of dead bodies are cynically used to gain more viewers" by news media "playing the same game of the horrific spectacle as ISIS", Kiwan contends, the collective's aim is "to show our common humanity and invite people to see us as human beings, not as Sunnis, Alawites, Christians, or Shiites" (interview with Bayoumi 2015; see also Abounaddara 2015, 2016; interview with Lenssen 2020).

Related co-operative initiatives have embraced the ethos of emergency cinema – or "vernacular video" in some renderings – as a form of documentary activism, one informed by a collective commitment to producing ethical, socially responsible counter-information (see also Jabbour et al. 2018; Mincheva 2020; Ruchel-Stockmans 2021; Snowdon 2014). In response to regime violence, "many young people took their video cameras and mobile phones as the alternative to a weapon, as an act of non-violence against authoritarianism", Wessels (2019) maintains. "Combined with the felt power of many, in street protests and defiance against regime violence, the camera became a symbol of hope, of resistance as a means of disruption" (2019, 176). Still, despite a range of important videos being produced and shared, primarily over YouTube and grass-roots news channels, the camera's effectiveness has been increasingly called into question over the years. "[I]nstead of a global solidarity", she believes, "the sheer number of videos of war and violence did not lead to the intended empathy but rather to audience fatigue with violence" (2019, 189). Concerns that the proliferation of images is diminishing their strength are similarly addressed by López (2021), whose analysis of Syrian cinema – including the documentary *Silvered Water, Syria Self-Portrait* with its remixing of vernacular Arab Spring videos found online – leads her to call for new cyberspaces to be created for "the free and open circulation of images" beyond "financial interests, power dynamics and structural monopolies" (2021, 13). Here López envisages these spaces being "built collectively" in accordance with the "principles of the digital commons and free culture", thereby inviting "the active participation of everyone" in an "infinite, interactive, global conversation online". The only way for images to gain political force, she concludes, is for filmmakers to speak "to the people, not in their name, and give them back their images" (2021: 13).

Weaponizing Imagery

Empowering efforts to establish the conditions for public dialogues about images, and in so doing instigate debate about reconfiguring relations of visuality – "the recognition of the right of every human being to a dignified image", in Abounaddara's (2015) terms – necessarily entails radically challenging the Syrian regime's evolving stratagems for consolidating visual hegemony. A vital dimension of its military's operation to reclaim territory from opposing forces has been the corresponding information war waged by state authorities, namely their success in weaponizing what amounts to a "post-truth" campaign to subvert the uprising's visually democratising narratives.

Countervailing image-tactics, suggestive of a visual iconography of militarism, have been operationalised by government officials, security agents, armed combatants and the like, present on the ground as well as in the virtual realm. An early example of the latter is the Syrian Electronic Army (SEA), which first surfaced in 2011. Government supporters, if not the Assad regime itself, were widely regarded to be behind the loosely organised grouping of online hackers and activists making up its membership. In declaring "cyberwar" intent on refuting the "fabricated news" broadcast by Arab and Western media, SEA described itself on its website as "a group of enthusiastic Syrian youths who could not stay passive towards the massive distortion of facts about the recent uprising in Syria" (cited in Fowler 2013; see also Zambelis 2012). Over the years, several denial-of-service attacks have been launched, websites defaced, graphic video footage posted, social media platforms such as Facebook spammed and high-profile hacks engineered, including into news organisations' Twitter accounts to send out false tweets (one asserting two White House explosions left President Obama injured triggered a major stock market devaluation in the US before it was corrected). "Our mission is to defend our proud and beloved country Syria against a bloody media war that has been waged against her", one of the pro-regime hackers, Th3 Pr0, boasted. "The controlled media of certain countries continues to publish lies and fabricated news about Syria" (interviewed by Katerji 2013). As perceptions this "information war" posed a serious threat grew, media platforms were increasingly subjected to fierce disputes between factions over the journalistic mediation of facticity.

Effecting control over precisely what counts as "truth" has been the primary objective of the Assad regime's disinformation campaign. For it to advance, public confidence in professional and citizen-activists' evidentiary images would have to be undermined at all costs. Amongst the strategies adopted, Hamad (2021) writes, is the appropriation of visual content "documenting the regime's own crimes, whilst re-narrating the story behind the images in order to recast victims of the regime as victims of anti-regime 'terrorists'" (2021, 64). Further, "a policy of defaming the reputation of Syria's democratic opposition" sought to ensure "any video or photographic images associated with them would be deemed untrustworthy and misleading", that is, rendered "into a state of social stigmatisation" (2021, 65). Equally significant, however, is what Hamad terms "the absence of image" tactic, which is intended to compensate for the regime's lack of evidentiary images to support its conspiracy narrative. This tactic plays out through key influencers supportive of this narrative, who contribute to rumour-making to cast doubt on oppositional imagery while, at the same time, online trolls seek to devalue this imagery as fakery on the discussion threads of Western news outlets, international human rights organisations, and the like (2021, 65–66; see also Matar 2019). In this climate, then, it is understandable why there can be no certainty such imagery, regardless of its evidentiary provenance, will elicit active responses from distant publics. "Violent images from Syria have entered a global economy in which images are consumed as part of a 'spectacle' of violence and indignity", Jabbour et al. (2018) maintain, "their proliferation an obstacle to visibility". Indeed, they add, even "when such images are used for advocacy, or for humanitarian mobilisation for support and funding, the plethora of images risks normalising Syrian deaths and blurs issues of justice and responsibility" (2018, 1; see also Chouliaraki 2015; Dencik and Allan 2017).

Promulgating confusion over what counts as credible imagery may alarm some, stoke fear in others, or educe indifference, even apathy in still others. "The difficulties of established journalism in Syria, coupled with the surge of new media in war coverage", Cosentino (2020) contends, "allowed for the emergence of conflicting narratives that essentially made the Syrian Civil War the first post-truth conflict of the twenty-first century". Over its first decade, "emotional and often unverifiable information supplanted rigorous and factual reporting, and competing interpretations of the events clashed constantly" (2020, 92). In contrast with investigations into authoritarianism focusing on how propaganda is wielded to legitimise violence and repressive control, Wedeen's (2019) analysis strives to understand how al-Assad's regime has undertaken to cultivate the ideological compliance of ordinary Syrians, encouraging them to align with rhetorics of order and stability. Instances of direct manipulation abound, but equally important is the strategic intent to produce and exploit heightened anxieties over truth, not only to undercut acts of resistance, but also to induce political indifference. While "the regime has not always been able to establish its own authority over the facts", she observes, "it has been repeatedly successful in sowing doubt among a variety of addressees about the nature of evidence as such and the credibility of oppositional narratives" (2019: 79). Divisive imagery generated by well-meaning citizen journalists and filmmakers, like the testimonial witnessing of activists, affords the regime opportunities to cast suspicion on news reporting otherwise regarded as trustworthy. That is, "an oversaturated high-speed information environment" can be made to engender moral ambiguities the circulation of information is intended to allay, Wedeen argues, such that ensuing "conditions of generalized uncertainty make it easy for people to find alibis for avoiding commitment to judgment at all" (2019, 79–80). To the extent narrow, self-confirming views of "siloed publics" invite ambivalence in response, it follows, the regime progresses its imperative to construct "a vision of national collectivity in which dissidence could be conflated with terrorism and the regime's violence valorized or ignored – or displaced onto the insurgent fighter" (2019, 159).

Or displaced onto Syrian refugees. It is estimated more than 6.6 million people have been forced to flee the country since 2011, with a similar number being internally relocated (UNHCR 2021). Activist demands for reform looked like they were finally gaining traction with Europe's politicians in September 2015, many of whom were responding to photographs taken by photojournalist Nilüfer Demir of a tragic scene on a Turkish beach, where the corpses of drowned Syrian refugees had washed ashore. In one of her photos, three-year-old Alan Kurdi was shown face down on the sand, while in another a Turkish police officer, who had recovered the child's lifeless body, tenderly cradled him in his arms. "It felt like the moment a crisis defined by abstract debates over ideology, statistics and terminology suddenly shifted to one about people", Jamie Fahey of *The Guardian* revealed at the time (cited in Allan 2017, 216). Over and again, Western commentators stressed how the images "humanized" a crisis that previously seemed remote and intangible, somehow not involving "real people" like "us". The words "this could have been my child" featured repeatedly in press coverage, while the re-mediation of the imagery captured and relayed via social media platforms – photocollages and memes of Kurdi's prone body photoshopped into alternative scenes, depicted in artwork, caricatures, graffiti murals and so forth – provoked ideological reflection and critique, as well as parody or satire, to pinpoint perceived inconsistencies, contradictions or outright hypocrisies in public responses.

Expectant beliefs the Kurdi images would prove to be a "tipping point" in "awakening" public consciences, much like politicians' assurances their governments would respond compassionately, were greeted with considerable scepticism, and rightly so as it soon transpired. Policymaking is proving inadequate to the challenge of addressing the structural violence underpinning the Syrian refugee crisis. At the same time, stereotypes of displaced populations derive their strength from fear and ignorance. Too many news organizations have failed to delve beneath the surface of events to challenge repertoires of stereotypical visions, to respect the right of the dispossessed to have their voices heard (Mortensen et al. 2017; Wilmott 2017). Responding to concerns that these images would not sustain collective action over time, Tima Kurdi, who was Alan's aunt, expressed her worry that her family's tragedy would be soon forgotten. "They're not terrorists. They're human beings", she said in a newspaper interview, before making a plea poignant in its simplicity: "I want the world to remember that picture" (cited in Omand 2015).

When indifference perpetuates inaction, it is not surprising that some photographers openly question the communicative power of imagery. "Today, with hindsight, and after ten years of this bloody war, in which hundreds of thousands of people have lost their lives, I have lost all hope of changing things through photography", the photojournalist Emin Özmen (2021) stated recently. Still, while his efforts to bear witness to the conflict (including "interrogations, torture, and even executions") and its ensuing humanitarian crisis have left him "deeply traumatized", Özmen is convinced "documenting conflicts is essential for history, for collective memory [to ensure] we don't forget what happened". Aware his presence in a warzone has been a personal choice, one denied to those who lived there, he made a conscious decision to realign his work accordingly. Turning his attention away from the conflict's military aspects, he has sought to prioritise recording its impact on ordinary people. Rather than producing "raw" images "recording violence that no one wanted to see", he now tries "to 'say' the same things", but in a more subtle, less graphic way. As he elaborated:

> After witnessing the violence suffered by Syrian civilians, many of whom were forced to become "refugees", it became important for me to document their fate. I tried to collect their stories and capture their experiences and feelings in a soft or sensitive way. It was in total opposition to the violence of my first images of the conflict.
>
> The lives of all these people, their stories, their destinies, were suspended in a state of "in-between" where expectation, hope, anxiety, confusion and anguish coexisted, collided, confining them to lives lived in a vague and confused state. The visual language I used to try and reflect this situation had to mirror these emotions. These later images are the antithesis of my photographs of the fighting.
>
> *Özmen 2021*

In privileging the affectivities of experience, Özmen believes, this alternative approach opens up opportunities for him to heal his private trauma through photography while simultaneously encouraging him to explore his imagery's capacity to galvanise positive responses. "I would say that photographing the refugee crisis was an important emotional challenge", he explains, "but that sometimes hope comes to me from that work, contrary to how I felt when I photographed the fighting in Syria".

Conclusions

The militarisation of Syria's protracted crisis continues, with no end in sight. The incipient ecology of visual reportage remains in flux, the shifting imperatives of digital convergence reconfiguring more traditional conceptions of journalistic truth-seeking and verification in a climate of profound uncertainty. "I can not comprehend how the war in Syria is still going on", the photojournalist Lynsey Addario (2020) acknowledges. "Maybe people just don't care? I don't know. I have to reassure myself that regardless, it's important to take these pictures and have a historical record of this time". As her self-reflection makes clear, compassion is important, but it is photography's capacity to capture material evidence that will inspire concerted action to instigate change.

Since the outset of the crisis, however, demands for social justice in Syria have been actively repudiated in acrimonious swirls of disinformation across social media networks within the country and around the globe, creating confusion and cultivating cynicism. As noted above, the evidentiary value of war photography is recurrently denied, its reportage dismissed as "fake" or "manipulated" by the Syrian regime, including by Bashar al-Assad himself, and its supporters. Hence the urgency of ongoing efforts to safeguard vernacular imagery, records and documents from state censorship, as well as from less overtly politicised restrictions, such as where social media platforms have ceased ensuring distribution in response to other priorities. An example of the latter is the pressing need to offset automated software used by YouTube to detect and remove war-related content on the grounds that it is objectionable. "It's not just videos that have been deleted, it's an entire archive of our life", Syrian activist Sarmad Jilane told AFP. "Effectively, it feels like a part of our visual memory has been erased" (cited in AFP 2021). Critical here is the rise of human rights collectives, such as Syrian Archive, working to gather, authenticate and preserve eyewitness testimonials. Its members are "positioning themselves as visual specialists that both mimic established institutional modalities and help offset the lack of clear visual standards and workflows across journalism, the law and political advocacy", Ristovska (2019) points out, thereby improving the prospects of these materials "playing evidentiary and forensic roles whether in UN investigations or possible ICC [International Criminal Court] prosecutions" (2019, 335 and 347; see also Al-Kahwati and Mannergren Selimovic 2021; Saber and Long 2017).

This chapter's mode of enquiry has sought to problematise certain timeworn truisms about war photography, particularly those prescribing normative ideals where facts can and should be separated from values in the interest of dispassionate relay. Closer inspection reveals acutely personal motivations give shape and direction to what is covered, how and why by those striving to redress evasions, lacunae and silences by uploading imagery from the ground. Whether it is a "professional" or "amateur" behind the lens, many of these individuals embody a collective ethos of commitment to exposing the agonies of suffering, and in so doing elicit searching questions concerning responsibility and accountability. To bear witness on behalf of those otherwise effectively rendered in/visible to distant publics is to recognise their pain and anguish while, at the same time, proclaiming their human rights. Photographers compelled to put their own lives on the line risk being turned into military targets, as we have observed in this chapter, and yet so many of them persevere. Necessity impels resilience, never more so than when securing ways to document the everyday violence of military rule is a matter of survival for a country's citizens.

Bibliography

Abounaddara. 2015. "The enemy is indifference." *Bomb Magazine*, November 4. Available at: https://bombmagazine.org/topics/journalism

Abounaddara. 2016. "We are dying: Take care of the right to the image." Available at: www.documenta14.de/en/notes-and-works/1523/we-are-dying-take-care-of-the-right-to-the-image

Addario, L. 2020. "A war photographer turns her lens back home." Interview with J. Alexander. *Geneva Solutions*, December 14. Available at: https://genevasolutions.news/peace-humanitarian/a-war-photographer-turns-her-lens-back-home

AFP. 2021. "'Visual memory': Activists in race to save digital trace of Syria war.' *France 24*, March 8. Available at: www.france24.com/en/live-news/20210308-activists-in-race-to-save-digital-trace-of-syria-war

Al-Ghazzi, O. 2014. "'Citizen journalism' in the Syrian uprising: Problematizing Western narratives in a local context." *Communication Theory* 24: 435–454.

Al-Kahwati, A. and J. Mannergren Selimovic. 2021. "Addressing atrocity in Syria: New challenges for transitional justice.' Swedish Institute of International Affairs. Available at: www.ui.se/globalassets/ui.se-eng/publications/ui-publications/2021/ui-paper-no.-2-2021.pdf

Allan, S. 2017. "Revisioning journalism and the 'pictures in our heads.'" In *Rethinking journalism again*, edited by C. Peters and M. Broersma, 216–230. London and New York: Routledge.

Bayoumi, M. 2015. "The Civil War in Syria is invisible: But this anonymous film collective is changing that.' *The Nation*, June 29. Available at: www.thenation.com/article/archive/the-civil-war-in-syria-is-invisible-but-this-anonymous-film-collective-is-changing-that/

Chouliaraki, L. 2015. "Digital witnessing in conflict zones: The politics of remediation." *Information, Communication & Society* 18, no. 11: 1362–1377.

CNN 2012. "Syrian state TV broadcasts 'confession' by detained citizen journalist." *CNN*, May 5. Available at: https://edition.cnn.com/2012/05/05/world/meast/syria-citizen-journalist/index.html

Cosentino, G. 2020. *Social media and the post-truth world order*. London: Palgrave.

Cottle, S., R. Sambrook, and N. Mosdell. 2016. *Reporting dangerously: Journalist killings, intimidation and security*. London: Palgrave Macmillan.

CPJ. 2013. "Ali Mahmoud Othman committee to protect journalists." Available at: https://cpj.org/data/people/ali-mahmoud-othman/

Della Ratta, D. 2018. *Shooting a revolution: Visual media and warfare in Syria*. London: Pluto Press.

Della Ratta, D. 2021. "Shooting 2011–2021: Violence, visibility, and contemporary digital culture in post-uprising and pandemic times." *Film Quarterly* 75, no. 2: 68–75.

Dencik, L. and S. Allan. 2017. "In/visible conflicts: NGOs and the visual politics of humanitarian photography." *Media, Culture & Society* 39, no. 8: 1178–1193.

Elias, C. 2017. "Emergency cinema and the dignified image: Cell phone activism and film-making in Syria." *Film Quarterly* 71, no. 1: 18–31.

Fowler, S. 2013. "Who is the Syrian Electronic Army?" *BBC News Online*, April 25. Available at: www.bbc.co.uk/news/world-middle-east-22287326

Guardian. 2021. "Editorial: The Guardian view on the Arab Spring, a decade on: A haunting legacy." *The Guardian*, January 29.

Hamad, M. 2021. "The absent image: Resisting erosion of public trust in Syrian activists' evidential visuality." In *Feminist visual activism and the body*, edited by B. Sliwinska, 62–74. New York: Routledge.

Harkin, J., K. Anderson, L. Morgan, and B. Smith. 2012. *Deciphering user-generated content in transitional societies: A Syria coverage case study*. Report by the Center for Global Communication Studies, Annenberg School for Communication, University of Pennsylvania. Available at: https://repository.upenn.edu/cgi/viewcontent.cgi?article=1001&context=cgcs_publications

Heras, N. A. 2012. "The revolution will be uploaded: Citizen journalism in Homs.' *FairObserver.com*, March 4. Available at: www.fairobserver.com/article/revolution-will-be-uploaded-citizen-journalism-homs

Howard, P. N. and M. M. Hussain. 2013. *Democracy's fourth wave? Digital media and the Arab Spring*. Oxford: Oxford University Press.

HRW. 2011. "'We've never seen such horror': Crimes against humanity by Syrian Security Forces." Human Rights Watch report, June. Available at: www.hrw.org/sites/default/files/reports/syria0611webwcover.pdf

HRW. 2015. "If the dead could speak: Mass deaths and torture in Syria's detention facilities." Human Rights Watch report. December 16. Available at: www.hrw.org/report/2015/12/16/if-dead-could-speak/mass-deaths-and-torture-syrias-detention-facilities

Jabbour, S., M. Gate, A. Sabouni, S. al-Batal, and Humans of Syria Network. 2018. "Rehumanising the Syrian conflict: Photographs of war, health, and life in Syria." *The Lancet* 391, no. 10126. DOI: https://doi.org/10.1016/S0140-6736(18)30662-7

Johnston, L. 2017. "Looking after Ibrahim: How journalists network, develop and safeguard relationships with citizen journalists and activists in Syria." *Journalism Practice* 11, no. (2–3): 195–212.

Kamber, M. 2011. "Photographing conflict for the first time." *The New York Times*, October 25. Available at: https://lens.blogs.nytimes.com/2011/10/25/young-in-libya/

Katerji, O. 2013. "The Syrian Electronic Army are at cyber war with anonymous.' *Vice.com*, April 4. Available at: www.vice.com/en/article/gqn4w9/the-syrian-electronic-army-hacked-the-bbc

Kiwan, C. 2014. "Cellphone war reporting dumbs down the truth." *Newsweek*, December 7. Available at: www.newsweek.com/cellphone-war-reporting-dumbs-down-truth-289763

Lenssen, A. 2020. "The filmmaker as artisan: An interview with the members of Abounaddara." *Third Text* 34, no. 1: 159–171.

Linfield, S. 2019. "Assad's Syria recorded its own atrocities: The world can't ignore them." *The New York Review*, February 9. Available at: www.nybooks.com/daily/2019/02/09/syrias-torture-photos-witness-to-atrocity/

López, G. H. 2021. "Notes on the role of the camera within a (virtual) war: The case of Silvered Water, Syria Self-Portrait." *Digital War*. https://doi.org/10.1057/s42984-020-00026-7

Lynch, M., D. Freelon, and S. Aday. 2014. "Blogs and bullets III. Syria's socially mediated Civil War." *Peaceworks* 91. Washington: United States Institute of Peace.

Macleod, H. and A. Flamand. 2012. "Syrian who filmed Colvin attack is held." *The Sunday Times*, April 1, 28.

Mast, J. and S. Hanegreefs. 2015. "When news media turn to citizen generated images of war." *Digital Journalism* 3, no. 4: 594–614.

Matar, D. 2019. "The Syrian Regime's strategic communication: Practices and ideology." *International Journal of Communication* 13: 2398–2416.

Mortensen, M., S. Allan, and C. Peters. 2017. "The iconic image in a digital age: Editorial mediations over the Alan Kurdi photographs." *Nordicom Review* 38, no. 2: 71–86.

Mincheva, D. 2020. "Cinematic Islamic feminism and the female war gaze: Reflections on Waad Al-Kateab's for Sama." *Alphaville: Journal of Film and Screen Media* 20: 54–70.

Mollerup, N. G. and M. Mortensen. 2020. "Proximity and distance in the mediation of suffering: Local photographers in war-torn Aleppo and the international media circuit." *Journalism* 21, no. 6: 729–745.

Omand, G. 2015. "Alan Kurdi's aunt: 'I want the world to remember that picture.'" *The Toronto Star*. December 26. Available at: www.thestar.com/news/canada/2015/12/26/alan-kurdis-aunt-i-want-the-world-to-remember-that-picture.html

Özmen, E. 2021. "Photographing Syria's Civil War and its ramifications." *MagnumPhotos*. Available at: www.magnumphotos.com/newsroom/photographing-syria-civil-war-ramifications/

Rawlings, N. 2012. "In memoriam: Rémi Ochlik, 1983–2012." *Time LightBox*, February 22. Available at: http://lightbox.time.com/2012/02/22/remi-ochlik/#1

Ristovska, S. 2019. "Human rights collectives as visual experts: the case of Syrian Archive." *Visual Communication* 18, no. 3: 333–351.

RWB. 2011. "Foreign media urged to take utmost care to protect local sources." *Reporters Without Borders*, November 15. Available at: https://rsf.org/en/news/foreign-media-urged-take-utmost-care-protect-local-sources

RWB. 2012. "Syrian citizen journalists and activists capture 2012 Netizen Prize." *Reporters Without Borders*, March 12. Available at: https://rsf.org/en/news/syrian-citizen-journalists-and-activists-capture-2012-netizen-prize

RWB. 2013. "Journalism in Syria: Impossible job?" *Reporters Without Borders*, November 6. Available at: https://rsf.org/en/reports/journalism-syria-impossible-job

RWB. 2019. "Well-known Syrian citizen-journalist probably died in detention in 2013." *Reporters Without Borders*, April 19. Available at: https://rsf.org/en/news/syria-well-known-syrian-citizen-journalist-probably-died-detention-2013

Ruchel-Stockmans, K. 2021. "From amateur video to new documentary formats: Citizen journalism and a reconfiguring of historical knowledge." In *Media and mapping practices in the Middle East and North Africa*, edited by A. Strohmaier and A. Krewani, 139–158. Amsterdam: Amsterdam University Press.

Saber, D. and P. Long. 2017. "'I will not leave, my freedom is more precious than my blood': From affect to precarity: Crowd-sourced citizen archives as memories of the Syrian war." *Archives and Records* 38, no. 1: 80–99.

Salama, V. 2012. "Covering Syria." *The International Journal of Press/Politics* 17, no. 4: 516–526.

Snowdon, P. 2014. "The revolution will be uploaded: Vernacular video and the Arab Spring." *Culture Unbound, Journal of Current Cultural Research* 6, no. 2: 401–429.

SOHR. 2021. "Total death toll." *Syrian Observatory for Human Rights*, June 1. Available at: www.syriahr.com/en/217360/

Taub, B. 2016. "The Assad files." *The New Yorker*, April 18. Available at: www.newyorker.com/magazine/2016/04/18/bashar-al-assads-war-crimes-exposed.

Tepperman, J. 2015. "Syria's President speaks: A conversation with Bashar al-Assad." *Foreign Affairs* 94, no. 2: 58–65.

Trombetta, L. 2012. "Altering courses in unknown waters: Interaction between traditional and new media during the first months of the Syrian uprising." *Global Media Journal: German Edition* 2, no. 1. URN: urn:nbn:de:gbv:547-201200128

UNHCR 2021. "Syria refugee crisis." *The UN Refugee Agency*, February 5. Available at: www.unrefugees.org/news/syria-refugee-crisis-explained/

Wall, M. and S. el Zahed. 2015. "Syrian citizen journalism: A pop-up news ecology in an authoritarian space." *Digital Journalism* 3, no. 5: 720–736.

Wardle, C., S. Dubberley, and P. Brown. 2014. "Amateur footage: A global study of user-generated content in TV and online news output.' A Tow/Knight Report. Tow Center for Digital Journalism, Columbia Journalism School. Available at: https://academiccommons.columbia.edu/doi/10.7916/D88S526V

Wedeen, L. 2019. *Authoritarian apprehensions: Ideology, judgement and mourning in Syria.* Chicago: University of Chicago Press.

Wessels, J. 2019. *Documenting Syria*. London: IB Tauris.

Wilmott, A. C. 2017. "The politics of photography: Visual depictions of Syrian refugees in U.K. online media." *Visual Communication Quarterly* 24, no. 2: 67–82.

Zambelis, C. 2012. "Information wars: Assessing the social media battlefield in Syria." *CTC Sentinel* 5, no. 7: 19–21. Available at: www.ctc.usma.edu/wp-content/uploads/2012/07/CTCSentinel-Vol5Iss75.pdf

4

SOCIAL MEDIA ICONS

Evidence and Emotion

Mette Mortensen

Icons are key to media coverage and popular memory of conflicts. During the mass media era, certain photojournalistic images came to stand for the Spanish Civil War, World War II, 9/11, etc. A "critical site of cultural memory" (Stallabrass 2017, 31), these simple, condensed representations were reproduced and spread, repurposed and appropriated to the extent that they became instantly recognisable to the wider public. Social media have over the past years left a distinctive mark on which images gain iconic status. Users of social media mass disseminate pictures from conflict areas, taken by professional and non-professional photographers alike. They have contributed significantly making icons out of, for example, the images of Neda Agha Soltan (2009) from the post-election uprising in Iran as well as the ones of Alan Kurdi (2015) and Omran Daqneesh (2016), both related to the civil war in Syria. The news media were initially reluctant to publish these images because they showed appallingly graphic scenes of children or young people that were suffering or death. However, they were included in mainstream news coverage after they had gone viral on social media.

This chapter explores what I conceptualise as "social media icons", an umbrella term for different forms of icons emerging through social media processes of production, dissemination and mobilisation as opposed to traditional photojournalistic icons published in the mass media. Scholars have studied patterns of mobilising icons across digital media platforms (e.g Assmann and Assmann 2010; Dahmen et al. 2018; Mortensen 2016; Olesen 2018; Stage 2011), the interplay between news media and social media (Mortensen 2015; Mortensen et al. 2017) as well as how users exert an influence on the meaning-making of icons by circulating critical, humorous memes and other appropriations (Boudana et al. 2017; Ibrahim 2016; Mortensen 2017; Olesen 2018). However, extant scholarship leaves us with the question unanswered as to how social media icons are made sense of by the public. This chapter posits that social media icons (as well as icons in general) are recurrently interpreted within

DOI: 10.4324/9781003176923-5

a framework of evidence and emotion. This overlooked aspect becomes particularly manifest in relation to social media icons of children in the context of conflict, which I, for the same reason, use as empirical examples in this chapter: Social media icons provide evidence of specific violations against this vulnerable group, while also showing children in an emotionally compelling way. On account of their simple expression and seemingly straightforward message, social media icons "… create the illusion of consensus" as Susan Sontag (2003, 5) has observed about photographs of war victims.

This chapter attempts to unravel the underlying complexity of social media icons through my framework "evidence and emotion". It begins with three theoretical sections, in which I first briefly present the concept social media icons, before developing the framework of evidence and emotion and introducing children war victims as a frequent motif for social media icons. In the following section, I analyse configurations of the evidence and emotion framework through two different forms of social media icons. They have been selected because they both stem from the Syrian Civil War and are cases major enough to have generated sufficient attention across media to enable study of the interplay between evidence and emotion. The first example is an "instant news icon" (Mortensen 2016) Omran Daqneesh, the boy depicted in an ambulance in Aleppo in 2016, which exemplifies how emotion is key to mobilising representations of child victims as icons and also how emotion at the same time triggers allegations that the imagery lacks evidence. As the second example, I analyse what I term an "iconic actor", the young girl Bana Alabed who achieved this status by delivering visual testimony through social media about the humanitarian catastrophe in Syria from 2016. This analysis demonstrates the intertwinement of evidence and emotion throughout the communication by and about Alabed. Finally, the conclusion reflects on how the application of the evidence and emotion framework forms changing patterns of consent and dissent that are key to understanding evidence and emotion in social media icons.

Social Media Icons

In the current era of image abundance, scholars have raised the question as to whether icons should be regarded as relics of the mass media epoch. Social media icons occur and fade faster than mass media icons, which tended only to be recognised as such after they had passed the test of time (see e.g. Hariman and Lucaites 2007). By this token, Stallabrass argues that "… iconic images cannot emerge in extremely saturated digital environments" (2017, 46). However, most scholars agree that the concept "icon" is still applicable to images generating mass traction on social media. This term enables us to recognise why and how political and cultural power is attributed to certain images and to understand this power against the historical backdrop of iconic imagery from the 20th century as well as existing conceptual and theoretical frameworks.

During the 1990s and 2000s, scholars focused on the ways in which iconic imagery published in mass media contributed to shaping public discourses in relation to political news (Bennett and Lawrence 1995), foreign policy (Perlmutter 1998), Holocaust memorialisation (Brink 2000) and liberal democracy (Hariman and Lucaites 2007). From the 2010s, research has attempted to grasp iconic images generated through social media, not least occasioned by major cases such as the social media icons Neda Agha Soltan (Assmann and Assmann 2010; Mortensen 2011; Stage 2011), Alan Kurdi (e.g. Dahmen et al.2018; Durham 2018; Mortensen and Trenz 2016; Olesen 2018) and Omran Daqneesh (Irom 2019; Mollerup and Mortensen 2020; Mortensen and Mollerup 2021). "Impromptu publics" form on social media fueled by strong and often fleeting emotional responses in an increasingly polarised political climate that intensely promote certain images or actors through likes, shares, comments, etc. (Mortensen 2016; Mortensen and Trenz 2016). From their social media origin, these icons spread to other platforms and are covered by mainstream news media, thus closing the gap between offline and online media as well as between professional and non-professional actors.

The Evidence and Emotion Framework

This chapter focuses on social media icons; however, it is important to acknowledge that the evidence and emotion framework can also be observed in the canonisation of mass media icons, including the World War II photo "Boy in the Ghetto" (1943) and Nick Ut's image of the Napalm-burned girl from the Vietnam War (1972). Naturally, this framework has undergone historical changes. In today's connective media circuit, images or actors are proclaimed to be icons instantaneously. "Boy in the Ghetto", by contrast, gained iconic status several years after the photo had been taken. Moreover, institutions fundamental to democracy, the court of law and the mass media, were key in turning "Boy in the Ghetto" into an icon, whereas new actors, that is, media users, grassroots organisations etc., also take part in promoting and contextualising social media icons within this framework.

Evidence and emotion intertwine in various ways as interpretive framework for social media icons. This framework attributes credibility on different levels. At times they are mutually re-enforcing, for instance, if the legal discourse vouches for the credibility of the social media icon in the sense of verification and works in tandem with the emotional credibility clinging to the immediacy and authenticity of the image. At other times, evidence and emotion steal authority from one another. Their entanglement can raise suspicion or lead to confusion, for example, their call for emotions might be regarded as undue bias distracting from their proof value or even as propaganda and fake news. In any event, this interplay between evidence and emotion is central to understanding how social media icons are ascribed meaning and exert an influence on the formation of public opinion.

To grasp why evidence and emotion are recurrently evoked as a framework for social media icons, it is beneficial to look into the tension between "authenticity" and "symbolization" characteristic of icons (Brink 2000; see also e.g. Alexander et al.2012; Hariman and Lucaites 2007; Mortensen 2013). Iconic images are at once authentic in that they are fixed to historical instances and symbolic as they are open for projected sentiments, beliefs, experiences, etc. By the same token, Boudana, Frosh and Cohen (2017, 1212) note that the broad social and moral significance of these representations "go beyond the referential meaning of the originally reported event", and Assmann and Assmann contend that when canonised as an icon "an *image of*" turns into "an *image for*" (2010, 235 italics in original). The authenticity of social media icons translates into discourses concerning the evidence they procure and the symbolicity into discourses about their emotional appeal. In the following, I present the two in turn.

Social Media Icons as Evidence

When "evidence" is used in connection with social media icons, this term alludes to either their (potential) function as legal proof or to the images providing testimony in a documentary or journalistic sense. Even though the implications of "evidence" obviously differ in the institutional settings of law and media, these two understandings of "evidence" often become discursively blurred. Connotations with legal institutions may be taken as promise of the truth value of an image regardless of whether it is used as formalised, juridical evidence or not. This builds on cultural constructions of photographic "realism" and "truth", which are historically rooted in the positivist paradigm of using the camera for legal purposes.

Icons have rarely been called upon as proof during court proceedings; a famous exception is the World War II imagery "Boy in the Ghetto". The photo shows an unknown Jewish boy in a group of people in the Warsaw Ghetto with his arms raised in response to a German soldier with a machine gun. It was taken by a similarly unknown Nazi photographer in 1943 to document the demolition of this Ghetto. During the International Military Tribunals in Nuremberg, 1945–1946, "Boy in the Ghetto" was among the 1,800 still photographs prepared as evidence (Abram 2003, 84), and it served as proof in the case against Corporal Josef Bloesche, the German soldier with the gun, who was sentenced to death (Zelizer 2010, 139). In connection with the trials in Nuremberg and later the televised one against Eichmann in Jerusalem in 1961, the photo caught the attention of the media and turned into a key World War II icon (Abram 2003; Raskin 2004; Zelizer 2010). While the use of icons as legal evidence is sparse, the connotations of juridical discourses still hold, and the word "evidence" is used in a way that erases the borderlines between legal, documentary and journalistic discourses. "Evidence" thus holds a performative capacity on how social media icons are perceived.

In the context of conflicts, "[p]hotographic evidence has become all but obligatory to demonstrate the fact of atrocity", as Judith Butler contends (2009, 70). The great public interest in icons magnifies some overall tendencies of photographic evidence. Soon after its invention in 1839, the promise of photography as evidence was recognised, and the police started systematically using the medium for identification and surveillance from the 1860s (e.g. Mnookin 1998; Porter and Kennedy 2012; Sekula 1986; Tagg 1988). This belongs to a paradigm shift in the second half of the 19th century "… bound up with the emergence of new institutions and new practices of observation and record-keeping" (Tagg 1988, 5). From the outset, the status of photography as evidence was controversial. Even though the camera was considered a scientific instrument for securing true and objective proof, it was also seen as a tool for manipulation that could lead to miscarriages of justice.

This controversy has left a decisive mark on how icons are regarded as evidence; their veracity is invariably up for debate, and they are habitually accused of being misinformative, manipulative or fake news. Examples abound of such debates, from Robert Capa's falling republican soldier (1936), to "Boy in the Ghetto" (1943), to Nick Ut's photograph from the Vietnam War of the Napalm-burned girl (1972). Recent examples include social media icons Neda Agha Soltan (2009), Alan Kurdi (2015), Omran Daqneesh (2016) and Bana Alabed (2016–). Discussions concerning their credibility attests to the uncertainty attached to photography as evidence and the great political stakes in icons.

As an integral part of current conflicts, social media icons are mobilised as evidence, and this generates polarised responses of support and condemnation. Today's ubiquity of smartphone cameras and easy access to circulating images facilitates a bottom-up infrastructure for "visible evidence-gathering" (Dencik and Allan 2017, 1179). Eyewitness footage recorded on a massive scale during conflicts has the potential to turn into iconic evidence. At the same time, as the analysis will show, the skepticism concerning icons as evidence has increased with the options for manipulating images, falsifying information about their contexts and fabricating deep fakes. Moreover, various institutions and actors have joined (and challenged) legacy media in carrying out fact-checking, for example, NGOs and online investigative initiatives such as Bellingcat and Syrian Archive.

Social Media Icons and Emotion

If we turn our attention to what Lene Hansen has designated "iconic emotionality" (2015, 270), icons have the ability to "concentrate and direct emotions" (Hariman and Lucaites 2007, 36) among large audiences. While observations about their emotional impact are mostly inferred from news coverage and public debate, user studies also confirm emotionality to be the dominant response to social media icons (e.g. Boudana et al. 2017; Mortensen and Trenz 2016). Emotional identification allows for immediate and seemingly unfiltered engagement:

> The emotional identification temporarily overcomes any sense of artificiality or awkwardness that comes from seeing the image as an image. Likewise, in a world lived among strangers, emotional resonance becomes an important measure of connection.
>
> *Hariman and Lucaites 2003, 61*

As Hariman and Lucaites underscore, emotion unites audiences and becomes a "measure" of the connection created by the icon. Media coverage of icons habitually refers to how they move and touch audiences. Much coverage of icons is meta-coverage. This tends to foreground the emotional aspect, which self-reinforcingly is often performed and reported on at the same time (Mortensen 2016).

Personification is essential to the emotional plea of icons, that is, a single individual, often a victim, standing for the collective and allowing the imagery to symbolise larger events and phenomena. As Kurasawa asserts:

> Personification is a representational genre that singles out a specific person's condition as a figurative and literal embodiment of the gravity or intensity of the suffering caused by a humanitarian crisis. It is created by a close-up shot of a single victim (or, occasionally, a small group of victims) who is portrayed in a state of raw, existential pain, often in isolation from others and in a manner that is stripped of any contextual information.
>
> *Kurasawa 2012, 72*

Victims are presented as more or less "universal", even if the icon emerges from a specific situation. In-between the single victim and all victims, the space opens for emotional identifications and investments.

Personification enables viewers to project their feelings onto the image. This is also used strategically to catch the attention of news audiences, encourage political action, mobilise humanitarian aid, etc. However, emotional identification comes at the cost of obscuring "… the geo/temporal locatedness" (Seu 2015, 655), and may be perceived as "humanitarian sentimentalism" (Kurasawa 2012, 207). All in all, iconic emotionality has both been pointed to as driver behind their mass appeal and criticised for simplifying and decontextualising.

Social Media Icons of Children

Social media icons of children constitute a conspicuous example of the evidence and emotion framework: These images carry a distinct emotional plea as evidence of violations against the vulnerable subjects. Children represent "ideal victims" (Seu 2015) but are also "complex and ambiguous" reflections of adult "hope and anxieties" (Al-Ghazzi 2019, 3227). Depicted as innocent, passive and exposed to adult aggression, they have traditionally signified essential civilian sacrifice and victimhood. Social media icons of children continue the tradition forming in the late 19th century and throughout the 20th century of using photography of war victims as evidence in media coverage, humanitarian communication and legal settings. The before-mentioned photograph "Boy in the Ghetto" is said to first institute the child war victim as motif for photojournalistic icons (Magilow and Silverman 2015, 13) and has been followed by the photograph from of the Napalm-burnt girl from the Vietnam War (1972), images of children the famines in Ethiopia and Sudan and the social media icons that we will shortly turn our attention to.

Iconic images of children "work on both affective and ethical levels, appealing to compassion and to a discourse of universal human rights", as Zarzycka (2016, 29) observes, thereby implicitly evoking the evidence and emotion framework.

They hold "such potency" in their call for solidarity that they turn into "the object of all our collective good intentions" (Frost and Stein, 1989, cited after Seu 2015, 655). On the other hand, iconic representations of children have repeatedly been criticised for simplified, strategic use of emotionality:

> Reducing complex issues to binaries consisting of good and evil, guilt and innocence, war and peace, images of children take emotional advantage of their audiences while serving the institutional interests of governments, NGOs, media corporations, and political parties.
>
> *Zarzycka 2016, 30*

Even though the photographs are used to document specific circumstances, children are usually depicted in isolation from the social structures of family and local environment as well as from cultural and political contexts. In the following, two examples of social media icons of children are analysed, *the instant news icon* Omran Daqneesh and *the iconic actor* Bana Alabad.

Emotion Taken as Lack of Evidence: Omran Daqneesh (2016)

In August 2016, the images of Omran Daqneesh cleared international front pages. The still photos and video of the three-year-old boy sitting injured in an ambulance after an airstrike was taken by several non-professional photographers in Aleppo and first posted on YouTube by the local media co-operation Aleppo Media Center (for details, see Mollerup and Mortensen 2020; Mortensen and Mollerup 2021). At this point, Aleppo was besieged, and civilians were hit by severe confrontations and bombardments. International media relied on local photographers to supply images, since it was deemed too dangerous for their own staff to report from Syria. The following analysis of Daqneesh is based on comparison of English-language coverage of this case from Western and pro-Assad news media, which a research assistant retrieved and collated. A total of 26 news articles were studied.

   Western news media only published the images of Daqneesh after they had gone viral, the coverage devoting attention to how the emotional outpour on social media had created an instantaneous icon through an "affective wind, rousing the urge to engage with the collective experience – each retweet, share, or comment functioned as an affective performance affirming the event as socially significant in the global public" (Demetriades 2020, 157). This suggests that while images or actors become icons on social media, established news media still play a great role in consolidating this status. Moreover, this also illustrates how news media often turn to meta-coverage of icons after social media impromptu publics have attributed this status to certain images. Only to a limited degree did this coverage convey factual information about the specific situation and present the political and social context. Personification was instrumental in the news coverage confirming the iconicity of this imagery. Declaring Daqneesh to be the "Face" of civilian suffering in Syria, coverage maintained that the boy in the ambulance was the emblem of thousands of innocent Syrian War victims (e.g. Shaheen 2016). This also became evident in a meta-story run in numerous media outlets about CNN anchor Kate Bolduan's high-emotional reporting:

> CNN anchor Kate Bolduan struggled to hold back tears Thursday while reporting an update on Omran Daqeesh [sic], a 5-year-old boy who was filmed and photographed moments after being pulled from his destroyed home in the aftermath of an airstrike on Aleppo, northern Syria. (…) After rolling footage of the boy's rescue, Bolduan reveals that the Daqeesh family survived the bombing, but that more than 250,000 people have been killed since the start of Syria's civil war in 2011.
> Then, the anchor appears to stop holding back her emotions.
> "What strikes me is we shed tears, but there are no tears here. He doesn't cry once. That little boy is in total shock. He's stunned," Bolduan says, voice wavering.
>
> *Russo 2016[1]*

Even if Bolduan connects the single victim to the "more than 250,000 people [...] killed", Daqneesh seems to be the primary trigger of emotions. When focusing on this war victim, "the anchor appears to stop holding back her emotions". Personification was similarly at play in the political response. For instance, US State Department spokesman John Kirby from the Obama administration emphasised that Omran was "the real face of what's going on in Syria" (Shaheen 2016), thus at once attributing the image symbolic value and stating that this was "real".

The emotional sway was also central to pro-Assad coverage, which, however, evaluated this negatively as symptom of the imagery's lack of evidentiary documentation. This coverage consistently dismissed the Daqneesh imagery as fake news and propaganda, fabricated to elicit emotion:

> Omran Daqneesh, a bewildered, injured child, extracted from the rubble in Aleppo, "the symbol of Syria's suffering," has been proven to be a propaganda heist, highlighting the exploitation of children as war advocacy tools.
>
> *Bartlett 2017*

Pro-Assad coverage, in this case from *Russia Today*, pointing to missing evidence is interesting considering the scarce attention Western news media paid to what the image factually documented. According to this coverage, the emotional appeal of the image was constructed to mobilise support for Western military intervention in Syria as "… part of a propaganda war, aimed at creating a 'humanitarian' excuse for Western countries to become involved in Syria", as *CCTV*, China's state broadcaster, explained (Dearden 2016). The value of the image as evidence was also reputed by a high-ranking Russian military source: "Major General Igor Konashenkov claimed images of the strike on Omran's family home indicated a blast less powerful than an air-fired missile and may have been caused by rebel mortars or IEDs" (Dearden 2016).

This interpretation was supported by witness testimony cited in numerous news media from the boy's father, Mohammad Kheir Daqneesh, who explained that his son, only slightly injured, had been staged as an iconic war victim without the family's knowledge or consent (e.g. Specia and Samaan 2017). The father also said that he had been pushed to blame the bombing on Russia and the Syrian regime. Western news media, on the other hand, asserted that the Assad-regime had pressured Mohammad Kheir Daqneesh into testifying in its favour.

In the reception of this instant news icon, the evidence and emotion framework is activated by the emotional aspect being highlighted straightaway. This is predictable considering how the great emotional response on social media has become a standardised narrative in iconisation processes. Western news coverage focused only marginally on what the image bore evidence to and turned instead to personification in proclaiming the boy to be the "Face" of Syria. Pro-Assad coverage, by contrast, attacked the emotional investment in this imagery for being a sign of lacking evidence. Even though emotions are – and always have been – central to iconisation processes, the validity of the instant news icon was discredited on this account. Instant news icons are particularly vulnerable to this criticism as they are born out of social media impromptu publics dominated by emotion rather than evidence. In this case, the opposing side answered back by re-contextualising this instant news icon through witnesses and experts vehemently disputing its authenticity as evidence.

Iconic Actors Arguing through Evidence and Emotion: Bana Alabed (2016–)

The interpretive framework of evidence and emotion has most recently been seen in relation to what I coin "iconic actors", that is, civilians, and especially children, in war zones using social media to share their experiences. Main examples are Syrian children Bana Alabed (born 2008, active since 2016) and Muhammed Najem (16 years old in 2019, active since 2018), who both report on the Syrian Civil War using Twitter as the primary communicative outlet. With an environmental agenda, Greta Thunberg also powerfully assumes the role of iconic actor.

Iconic actors are obviously not iconic in the same sense as iconic images. Nonetheless, I find it pertinent to place them in the historical trajectory of icons to pinpoint continuities and changes: They strongly evoke the framework of evidence and emotion and draw on the well-established iconography of children personifying civilian suffering. At the same time, this framework is reconfigured by these active and empowered actors, who mark a decisive historical change from the notion of children as passive, "ideal victims" (Seu 2015). While emotional investment in instant news icons is enabled by their detachment from the specific circumstances, iconic actors make emotional pleas to the public based on their embodied and situated experience of war. In this way, they become performative subjects claiming rights, as Leurs (2017) observes more broadly. This accords with the general development within humanitarian communication that representations of competent children appealing for rights increasingly supplement the traditional figure of the victimised child devoid of agency (e.g. Wells 2008, 235).

Amongst the many civilians transmitting eyewitness testimonies from Aleppo in fall of 2016, Alabed was singled out as the personification of the Syrian war victim, and the news media soon declared her to be "an icon". Alabed, then seven years old, started tweeting about the humanitarian crisis befalling her family and other civilians in Aleppo from 24 September 2016. With the help of her mother, she reported in images and words on the suffering and damage in her local community and appealed to an international public for help. The mainstream news media closely followed the compelling story of the family's hardship and subsequent flight. Her image tweets initially gained worldwide attention because they invited "empathetic identification" (García 2017, 139) by providing an exclusive insight into the Syrian war from a child's perspective. Since living in asylum in Turkey from late 2016, Alabed has assumed the role of refugee activist, disseminating images of war victims and advocating peace, while also meeting celebrities and walking the red carpet at the Oscars.

There might be an element of chance in which cases attract attention and become defining for how a conflict is framed. However, the case of Alabed demonstrates that inter-iconicity (Hansen 2015, 269) often has an impact, which manifested itself here in the reference to the well-established motif of the "ideal" child war victim as well as her "commodity status as a young girl" (García 2017, 137). Along these lines, Alabed was repeatedly claimed to be "our era's Anne Frank" (e.g. Madani 2017, see also Chouliaraki and Al-Ghazzi 2022). Establishing the inter-iconic connection to Anne Frank, the most significant predecessor to her as iconic actor, emphasises Alabed's symbolic significance as a personification of Syrian war victims, an emotional, mythologised fixpoint in the incessant news stream from this conflict. Alabed herself acknowledges this personification, for instance, in a tweet of 23 June 2018: "Tonight i had the honour of receiving the freedom award. This award is for the millions of children who the world couldn't give them freedom".[2]

In the following, I focus on how evidence and emotion intertwine in Bana Alabed's own communication and the media coverage of her. She frequently disseminates graphic images of gravely wounded or dead Syrian children as visual documentation for war crimes, which she condemns with strong emotional undertones in the accompanying tweets. Her vehement criticism of the misconduct she claims to offer visual evidence of is unmistakable, for example, in a tweet from 5 May 2019: "Children are the saddest thing about the war in Syria. Very very big crimes against children. Those who start war where there are children are criminals. #Idlib"[3]

The evidence and emotion framework also infiltrates media coverage of Alabad. Most notably, we see how the credibility attached to these discourses become blurred as the emotion aimed at her persona was attacked by renouncing her credibility in terms of the evidence delivered. On the one hand, the emotional perspective was very visible, as García remarks:

> … the emotional investment triggered by first-person child narration is central to processes of social advocacy, and how the visual impact of still and moving images has the power to move audiences worldwide at a very rapid pace thanks to the digital paradigm.
>
> *García 2017, 134*

On the other hand, the reception of Bana Alabed also confirms the pattern that icons are contested for lack of evidence. As already mentioned, this accusation has accompanied icons since the mass media era. While veracity and factuality are obviously valid and grave concerns, this standard contestation of icons is also ascribable to the power icons hold on framing and shaping the media narrative about a given conflict. In this case, serious doubts have repeatedly been raised about the factual accuracy of the information disseminated by Alabed and about her identity, that is, whether this child was only working with herself and her mother or whether Bana Alabed was a cover-identity for terrorists or other actors propagating disinformation. As Al-Ghazzi remarks about the "digital witness" child in general, Alabed was "…simultaneously hyped up as the ultimate truth teller and/or dismantled as an intrinsically helpless victim of manipulation" (Al-Ghazzi 2019, 3226, see also Chouliaraki and Al-Ghazzi 2021). For example, when asked in an interview about whether he "trust[ed] her as an eyewitness", Syrian president Assad stated:

> You cannot build your political position or stand, let's say, according to a video promoted by the terrorists or their supporters. It's a game now, a game of propaganda, it's a game of media.
>
> *Syria Times 2017*

The mistrust in Alabed was repudiated by Bellingcat. This organisation specialised in online investigation through open-source fact-checking, devoted a lengthy report to testing Alabed's identity and credibility. Concluding that her identity was genuine and the information on Twitter accurate, the report stated that the "[c]riticism of Bana's account is rife with deliberate misunderstanding, misinformation, and lack of evidence" (Waters 2016).

Three crucial points crystallize from the case of Bana Alabed regarding the framework of evidence and emotion. First, as iconic actor, she herself communicates within this framework when making emotional pleas for humanitarian aid and political intervention. Second, credibility connects evidence and emotion and is key to negotiating her iconic status. The credibility ascribed to her figure as an emotional fixpoint was attacked by disputing the credibility of the evidence provided by her witness testimonies. Third, new actors assess and contextualise the value of iconic material as proof; Bana Alabed emerged as a viral phenomenon, and the online organisation Bellingcat performed the role of vetting her authenticity.

Conclusion: Patterns of Consent and Dissent

This chapter has explored the framework of evidence and emotion as a heavily politised aspect of social media icons. Sometimes evidence and emotion mutually reinforce one another. At other times, they are in conflict. Generally speaking, a phase of consent unfolds when the iconic status is established, and a phase of dissent takes place when the validity of the iconic status and the associated values, interpretations and political calls for actions are contested. The interplay between evidence and emotion in the initial phase enables the represented child to be mobilised as personification of suffering civilians. While the iconic imagery or actor is proclaimed to provide evidence of these injustices, the opposing fronts are predisposed to disagree on who is responsible for this agony. This, in turn, means that the iconic image or actor is thrown into doubt and the emotional appeal is interpreted as a sign of lacking evidence.

The analysis also points to how images or actors are proclaimed to be icons instantaneously in today's connective media circuit. They are attributed iconic status in social media and news media by highlighting the emotional impact inherent in their personification of the innocent child war victim. This became point of departure for the routine contestation of iconic representations, which in both instances was articulated as a fake news framing. While icons have always been accused of falsification, the children themselves and their families became directly involved in this battle for determining what the images provide evidence of. This manifested itself not least in regard to Alabed, who incarnates a decided break with the way in which children have typically been depicted as innocent and passive victims. As an iconic actor, she inhabits the triple role of, first, personifying the innocent victim, second, reporting from the war in her local surroundings, and, third, using her media platform for advocacy and activism. This renders personification more difficult, because she does not conform to the role of the passive actor to which general feelings of outrage, compassion, etc. can be projected.

Social media icons may appear to be a contradiction of terms. Why attach so much significance to a single image or actor when abundant images are spread and scattered on social media by the hour? Social media icons in a sense conform to the old script of iconic images that has been rehearsed and refined from the first half of the 20th century: Certain images are mobilised as bearers of condensed meanings; they impact public opinion and political discussions. They are also decisive for how a conflict is represented and remembered as "vehicles of memory" to use Barbie Zelizer's (2004) concept. They enter political battles concerning information, disinformation and misinformation, concerning which truth and whose truth they substantiate. At the same time, they break with this script in that they are often ephemeral and emerge outside of the media institutions and political establishments that have traditionally been key in determining the visual framing of conflicts. The social media icons studied in this chapter have materialised within hours rather than days through the intricate interplay between social media images and conflicts, generated by the active participation of civilians on the war-torn streets of Syria and online, sustained by political interests and spread according to algorithmic logics.

Notes

1 Omran Daqneesh was mainly described as five years old at the time this image went viral. However, later interviews indicate that he was three or four years old at the time of the attack in August 2016 (Mortensen and Mollerup 2021).
2 https://twitter.com/AlabedBana/status/1010650032318615552 (link accessed December 9, 2021).
3 https://twitter.com/AlabedBana/status/1125112355594092549 (link accessed December 9, 2021).

Bibliography

Abram, D. P. 2003. "The suffering of a single child: Uses of an image from the holocaust." Cambridge: Harvard.

Alexander, J. C., D. Bartmanski, and B. Giesen. 2012. *Iconic power: Materiality and meaning in social life*. New York: Palgrave Macmillan.

Al-Ghazzi, O. 2019. "An archetypal digital witness: The child figure and the media conflict over Syria'. *International Journal of Communication* 13: 3225–3243.

Assmann, A. and C. Assmann. 2010. "Neda—the career of a global icon." In *Memory in a global age: Discourses, practices and trajectories*, edited by A. Assmann and S. Conrad, 225–242. Basingstoke: Palgrave Macmillan.

Bartlett, E. 2017. "Absurdities of Syrian War propaganda." *RT*, November 2. Available at: www.rt.com/op-ed/408618-syria-war-propaganda-media-west/

Bennett, L. W. and R. G. Lawrence. 1995. "News icons and the mainstreaming of social change." *Journal of Communication* 45, no. 3: 20–39.

Boudana, S., P. Frosh, and A. A. Cohen. 2017. "Reviving icons to death: When historic photographs become digital memes." *Media, Culture & Society* 39, no. 8: 1210–1230.

Brink, C. 2000. "Secular icons: Looking at photographs from Nazi Concentration Camps." *History and Memory* 12, no. 1: 135–150.

Butler, J. 2009. *Frames of war: When is life grievable?* London: Verso.

Chouliaraki L, Al-Ghazzi O. 2022. Beyond verification: Flesh witnessing and the significance of embodiment in conflict news. *Journalism* 23 no 3: 649–667.

Dahmen, N. S., N. Mielczarek, and D. D. Perlmutter. 2018. "The influence-network model of the photojournalistic icon." *Journalism & Communication Monographs* 20, no. 4: 264–313.

Dearden, L. 2016. "Omran Daqneesh: China state media calls harrowing images of injured Syrian boy 'part of Western Propaganda War.'" *Independent*, August 23. Available at: www.independent.co.uk/news/world/middle-east/omran-daqneesh-photo-video-aleppo-boy-syria-injured-china-state-media-western-propaganda-war-a7205296.html

Demetriades, S. Z. 2020. "Cosmopolitan dimensions of virality and 'The Boy in the Ambulance.'" *Western Journal of Communication* 84, no. 2: 148–167.

Dencik, L. and S. Allan. 2017. "In/Visible conflicts: NGOs and the visual politics of humanitarian photography." *Media, Culture & Society* 39, no. 8: 1178–193.

Durham, M. G. 2018. "Resignifying Alan Kurdi: News photographs, memes, and the ethics of embodied vulnerability." *Critical Studies in Media Communication* 35, no. 3: 240–258.

García, A. B. 2017. "Bana Alabed: Using Twitter to draw attention to human rights violations." *Prose Studies* 39, no. (2–3): 132–149.

Hansen, L. 2015. "How images make world politics: International icons and the case of Abu Ghraib." 41, no. 2: 263–288.

Hariman, R. and J. L. Lucaites. 2003. "Public identity and collective memory in U.S. iconic photography: The image of 'Accidental Napalm.'" *Critical Studies in Media Communication* 20, no. 1: 35–66.

Hariman, R. and J. L. Lucaites. 2007. *No caption needed: Iconic photographs, public culture, and liberal democracy*. Chicago: University of Chicago Press.

Ibrahim, Y. 2016. "Tank man, media memory and Yellow Duck Patrol." *Digital Journalism* 4, no. 5: 582–596.

Irom, B. 2019. "Mediating Syria's strangers through Levinas: Communication ethics and the visuals of children." *Communication Theory* 29, no. 4: 441–462.

Kurasawa, F. 2012. "The making of humanitarian visual icons: On the 1921–1923 Russian Famine as foundational event." In *Iconic power: Materiality and meaning in social life*, edited by J. C. Alexander, D. Bartmanski, and B. Giesen, 67–84. New York: Palgrave Macmillan.

Leurs, K. H. A. 2017. "Communication rights from the margins: Politicising young refugees' smartphone pocket archives." *The International Communication Gazette* 79, no. (6–7): 674–698.

Madani, D. 2017. "7-Year-old refugee who tweeted during Aleppo Siege is writing a memoir." *Huffpost*, June 8. Available at: www.huffpost.com/entry/7-year-old-refugee-who-twee ted-during-aleppo-siege-is-writing-a-memoir_n_58ee4779e4b0f392747482b8

Magilow, D. H. and L. Silverman. 2015. *Holocaust representations in history: An introduction*. London: Bloomsbury Publishing Plc.

Mnookin, J. L. 1998. "The image of truth: Photographic evidence and the power of analogy." *Yale Journal of Law & the Humanities* 10, no. 1: 1–74.

Mollerup, N. G. and M. Mortensen. 2020. "Proximity and distance in the mediation of suffering: Local photographers in war-torn Aleppo and the international media circuit." *Journalism* 21, no. 6: 729–745.

Mortensen, M. 2011. "When citizen photojournalism sets the news agenda: Neda Agha Soltan as a Web 2.0 icon of post-election unrest in Iran." *Global Media and Communication* 7, no. 1: 4–16.

Mortensen, M. 2013. "The making and remakings of an American icon: Raising the flag on Iwo Jima from photojournalism to global, digital media." In *Eastwood's Iwo Jima: Critical engagements with flags of our fathers and letters from Iwo Jima*, edited by R. Schubart and A. Gjelsvik, 15–35. New York: Columbia University Press.

Mortensen, M. 2015. *Journalism and eyewitness images: Digital media, participation, and conflict*. New York: Routledge.

Mortensen, M. 2016. "'The image speaks for itself' – or does it? Instant News Icons, Impromptu Publics, and the 2015 European 'refugee crisis.'" *Communication and the Public* 1, no. 4: 409–422.

Mortensen, M. 2017. "Constructing, confirming, and contesting icons: The Alan Kurdi imagery appropriated by #humanitywashedashore, Ai Weiwei, and Charlie Hebdo." *Media, Culture & Society* 39, no. 8: 1142–1161.

Mortensen, M., S. Allan, and C. Peters. 2017. "The iconic image in a digital age: Editorial mediations over the Alan Kurdi photographs." *Nordicom Review* 38, no. S2: 71–86.

Mortensen, M. and N. G. Mollerup. 2021. "The Omran Daqneesh imagery from the streets of Aleppo to international front pages: Testimony, politics and emotions." *Global Media and Communication* 17, no. 2: 261–277.

Mortensen, M. and H. Trenz. 2016. "Media morality and visual icons in the age of social media: Alan Kurdi and the emergence of an impromptu public of moral spectatorship." *Javnost* 23, no. 4: 343–362.

Olesen, T. 2018. "Memetic protest and the dramatic diffusion of Alan Kurdi." *Media, Culture & Society* 40, no. 5: 656–672.

Perlmutter, D. D. 1998. *Photojournalism and foreign policy: Icons of outrage in international crises*. Westport: Praeger.

Porter, G. and M. Kennedy. 2012. "Photographic truth and evidence." *Australian Journal of Forensic Sciences* 44, no. 2: 183–192.

Raskin, R. 2004. *A child at gunpoint: A case study in the life of a photo*. Aarhus: Aarhus University Press.

Russo, C. H. 2016. "CNN anchor moved to tears during report on bloodied Syrian boy." *Huffpost*, August 19. Available at: www.huffpost.com/entry/cnn-kate-bolduan-tears-syr ian-boy_n_57b66abee4b03d51368789b9

Sekula, A. 1986. "The body and the archive." *October* 39, (Winter): 3–64.

Seu, I. B. 2015. "Appealing children: UK audiences' responses to the use of children in humanitarian communications." *The International Communication Gazette* 77, no. 7: 654–667.

Shaheen, K. 2016. "I filmed the Syrian boy pulled from the rubble – His wasn't a rare case." *The Guardian*, August 16. Available at: www.theguardian.com/world/2016/aug/18/i-fil med-the-syrian-boy-pulled-from-the-rubble-his-wasnt-a-rare-case

Sontag, S. 2003. *Regarding the pain of others*. London: Penguin Books Ltd.

Specia, M. and M. Samaan. 2017. "Syrian boy who became image of Civil War reappears." *The New York Times*, June 6. Available at: www.nytimes.com/2017/06/06/world/middlee ast/omran-daqneesh-syria-aleppo.html

Stage, C. 2011. "Thingifying Neda: The construction of commemorative and affective thingifications of Neda Agda Soltan." *Culture Unbound* 3, no. 3: 419-438.

Stallabrass, J. 2017. "Memory and icons: Photography in the war on terror." *New Left Review* no. 105: 29–50.

Syria Times. 2017. "The Syria Times online, 5 years on!" *Syriatimes. Sy*, October 3. Available at: http://syriatimes.sy/index.php/editorials/commentary/32859-the-syria-times-online-5-years-on

Tagg, J. 1988. *The burden of representation: Essays on photographies and histories*. Basingstoke: Macmillan Education.

Waters, N. 2016. "Finding Bana – Proving the existence of a 7-year-old girl in Eastern Aleppo." *Bellingcat*, December 14. Available at: www.bellingcat.com/news/mena/2016/ 12/14/bana-alabed-verification-using-open-source-information/

Wells, K. 2008. "CHILD SAVING OR CHILD RIGHTS: Depictions of children in international NGO campaigns on conflict." *Journal of Children and Media* 2, no. 3: 235–502.

Zarzycka, M. 2016. "Save the child: Photographed faces and affective transactions in NGO Child Sponsoring Programs." *The European Journal of Women's Studies* 23, no. 1: 28–42.

Zelizer, B. 2004. "The voice of the visual in memory." In *Framing public memory*, edited by K. R. Phillips, 157–186. Tusaloosa: The University of Alabama Press.

Zelizer, B. 2010. *About to die: How news images move the public*. Oxford: Oxford University Press.

5

EMBODIED PROTESTS ON SOCIAL MEDIA

The Visual Political Discourses of Vulnerability and Endurance in the Cases of "Hands Up, Don't Shoot" and #IRunWithMaud

Bolette B. Blaagaard

Within the space of six years, Michael Brown in 2014 and Ahmaud Arbery in 2020 were killed by white men in seemingly vigilante style incidents. Brown was 18 years old when he was killed by police officer Darren Wilson in Ferguson, Missouri, and Arbery was 25 when he was chased, trapped and killed by Travis McMichael, his father Gregory McMichael and their friend William "Roddie" Bryan in Georgia. Despite the differences in circumstances, both killings are associated with the continued struggle for civil rights in the United States, led recently, particularly, by the activist group named Black Lives Matter (BLM). Brown and Arbery were both unarmed and both were shot for no apparent, justifiable reason. Both men were African American and their deaths were captured on mobile devices, which circulated on social and legacy media, bringing visibility and supporting growing calls for protest and change in policing strategies and legal structures, such as Stand Your Ground.[1] The cases of Brown and Arbery are also similar in the way they were received by the public and in the digital and embodied protests they enabled on- as well as offline, which is the focus of this chapter.

This chapter takes as a starting point the two artifacts of engagement (Clark 2016) and embodied gestures – "Hands up, don't shoot" and "#IRunWithMaud" – that, respectively, accompanied the killings of Brown and Arbery as forms of protest. The chapter explores the entanglement of embodied gestures and digital protest imagery and expressions and asks what implications this entanglement poses to the political discourses it produces. As digital protest and online activism continue to be the focus of media scholarship and of importance to global politics, the embodied implications of the visual and discursive expressions have received less attention. The emphasis placed on the double nature of online expressions aims to address this gap in the scholarship. Theoretically, the chapter begins by arguing for the importance of protest images to the production of differing and diverse discursive formations

DOI: 10.4324/9781003176923-6

of publics. In the following section, I discuss how embodiedness presents itself as political acts in protest imagery forming counter-publics (Blaagaard 2019). I illustrate the theories by performing visual discursive analyses (Rose 2016) of selected digital gestural expressions from social media platforms and other online communication that display the political slogan and hashtag of "Hands up, don't shoot" and "#IRunWithMaud". I argue that the embodied slogan and hashtag are political acts that rupture socio-historical structures (Isin and Nielsen 2008) and produce spaces of appearance (Mirzoeff 2017). That is to say that the combination of digital and embodied political acts produces *double hashtags* that generate critical memory and a black public sphere (Baker 1994) enabled through a black gaze (hooks 2015). Circulating on social media platforms, the double hashtags and the accompanying visuals are produced and produce, in turn, a "regime of visibility" (Chouliaraki and Stolic 2017) or a "complex of visuality" (Mirzoeff 2011), which help determine the frames through which we perceive reality and public belonging (Blaagaard et al. 2017). Moreover, the political acts created by the double hashtags are not a monolith but produce two distinct political discourses through their digital and material manifestations: one of vulnerability and one of endurance.

Protest Images and Publics

Images of conflict and protest hold great sway over how societies are viewed and how history is told: Determining who is the victim and who is the perpetrator in the image means evaluating the political and social structures of the society in which protests take place. Iconic images of conflict or protest situations moreover show us who the intended viewing audience of the images are and how they perceive their own role in the conflict (Hariman and Lucaites 2007, Berger 2011). In other words, images of conflict and protest construct discursive publics (Warner 2002).

In their different ways, the two publications by, respectively, Robert Hariman and John Luis Lucaites (2007) and Martin A. Berger (2011) make this point. Taking as a starting point the image of the lone, Chinese protester facing down a row of military tanks in Tiananmen Square in 1989, Hariman and Lucaites (2007) argue that the image indirectly tells the intended spectators that they, the American viewing audience, and their liberal and deliberate consumer public, are politically more advanced than the Chinese. The message is produced through the perspective and framing of the image that points to a universalisation of the protest, according to Hariman and Lucaites (2007, 208–242; see also Blaagaard 2019, 256). They argue that liberalism's perceived opportunities for individuals to pursue happiness is translated into consumerism, that is, the freedom to buy items, brands and identities (Warner 1992) and is asserted as the pinnacle of political and social community development. The public that is called into being by the iconic image is a unified, American consumer public.

Despite the fact that no images of either the Civil Rights Movement or the feminist movement are among Hariman and Lucaites' top ten iconic images that they analyse and discuss in their seminal book, *No Caption Needed*, Berger insists that iconic images from the Civil Rights' struggle in the 60s do exist. Berger's examples include photos taken from the sit-ins at lunch counters in racially segregated Mississippi in 1963, Rosa Park being fingerprinted in Alabama in 1956 and the images of police dogs attacking protesters in Alabama in 1963. These images, which were selected for the pages in northern states' newspapers and journals, stand out for their focus on white agency, argues Berger. The images portray how white people harassed the black people who were quietly insisting on being served at the lunch counter; how a white police officer pressed Rosa Parks' fingers against the ink pad and how other white police officers unleashed their dogs on the peaceful protesters. An image in *Life* showing protesters being hosed down by the police is tellingly accompanied by a headline that reads "They fight a fire that won't go out" (Berger 2011, 15). This headline is clearly addressing a white public by positioning the firefighters as the agents, not the protesters. The images, Berger asserts, were chosen for the white readers of US newspapers in order for the white public to feel safe and in control, while simultaneously being able to support the struggle against segregation from afar. The African American population was portrayed as righteous, harmless and in need of white help. Arguably, this particular address to a white public is partly what grants the images their iconic status (Blaagaard 2019).

The work by Hariman and Lucaites and by Berger present us with two different arguments for the relationship between images of conflict and protest and the production of publics: (1) iconic images produce the unifying, deliberative but abstract public and (2) iconic images reproduce an exclusionary public focusing on the experiences and privileges of the white population. The difference between the two arguments is not surprising when looking at Hariman and Lucaites' own definition of iconic images (Hariman and Lucaites 2007, 30–34). They put forth a definition, which stresses the aesthetic *familiarity* of the image, the support of representational *conventions*, *performativity*, semiotically transcription of *social codes* and *emotionality*. Even the depiction of crises, which to Hariman and Lucaites is also part of an iconic image, only serves to reaffirm the convention in order to turn the representation into an abstract universality. These factors allow the spectator to engage in civic performance and to reproduce the familiar public, while making it difficult to interject with other(ed) or *un*familiar positions and experiences. In images as well as in classic theory of the public sphere, *the* public is premised on a narrative which brackets off differences, relying on unmarked, but white, male experience (Habermas 1989; Fraser 1991; Warner 1992, 2002). Thus, the

> "iconic" photographs endlessly reproduced in the newspapers and magazines of the period [of the Civil Rights era], and the history books that followed, were selected [because] they stuck to a restricted menu of narratives that performed reassuring symbolic work.
>
> *Berger 2011, 6*

This symbolic work reflected the familiarity of the dominant public transmitted through social codes of experienced conventions that privileged the white population.

In turn, from an abstract position of whiteness such a public may simply seem unifying and praised, because of the "normality" it exudes. As Warner (1992, 383) argues: "The bourgeois public sphere has been structured from the outset by a logic of abstraction that provides a privilege for unmarked identities: the male, the white, the middle class, the normal". Given the white hegemony of western culture, the reproduction and familiarity needed for an iconic image to emerge cannot help but reproduce an address to a public which was originally envisioned as *the* public, that is, the white population (Blaagaard 2019, 249–252). Arguably, social media and digitalisation of images democratise access and availability of amplification for diverse perspectives and voices. However, if regimes of visibility structure, "produce and regulate the public dispositions by which we collectively take responsibility of the plight of distant others" (Chouliaraki and Stolic 2017, 1172), they are nevertheless "ultimately informed by symbolic strategies of dehumanisation" (ibid. 1173), be they digital or analogue. Mette Marie Roslyng and Bolette B. Blaagaard (2020, 6) argue that it is "the discursive connections to the embodied and political realm" that make social media political and eventually may make "the boundaries of 'who speaks' [...] become permeable" (Chouliaraki and Stolic 2017, 1174). Summing up, images of protests may shock and disrupt, however, more often than not they also reproduce the "norm" and the familiar public by means of selected address and agency. Race relations in the United States may serve as an extreme but critical case of this.

Embodiedness and Political Acts

If the dominant public to Berger and Nicolas Mirzoeff, among others, is reproduced through iconicity as a white, male and middle class space, counter-publics may be understood to be supported by different kinds of visual expressions. These expressions are political acts that rupture socio-historical structures (Isin and Nielsen 2008, 10) and produce spaces of appearance (Mirzoeff 2017). Engin Isin and Gregg Nielsen (2008, 11) argue that political acts are a form of speech acts that produce citizens as acting subjects beyond the legal and dominant liberal framework of citizenship and the public sphere. While *the* public, as discussed by Warner (1992), heralds the abstraction of self, the counter-public or spaces of appearance are produced *by* the people and *for* the people – be they legal citizens or not. Berger refers to the images of counter-publics as "lost" or "missing" (Berger 2011, 112–156) from the dominant public. One of these missing images is of the 14-year-old boy, Emmett Till, who was lynched in Mississippi in 1955. His open casket was on display following his mother's wishes and the images of his mutilated face were published in black newspapers and circulated widely, because "the act of looking, specifically, looking at photographs of Till, [was credited with] the power to heal American race relations" (Berger 2011, 133). But while the images represented a call to action for the young black communities to an extent that produced the "Emmett Till generation" (ibid. 128), the images did not motivate the white public in a similar way. This was due to the united white press' "*disinclination* to see [the images] reproduced" (ibid. 133, italics in original). Berger argues that while the white press was traditionally divided into liberal and conservative publications nei-ther fraction found the images of Till relevant to their readers, because they would "have produced more unambiguously progressive results than the circulation of any other period photograph of white-on-black violence" (ibid.). Although they posed a potential for radical, social change, the images remained lost and unre-deemed. Other lost or missing images are of African American agency, such as images of black women fighting back against police violence, the black power salute performed by members of the Black Panther Party (BPP) at the Olympic Games in 1968, and the seated position of BPP leader Huey P. Newton, "showing [him] armed with Zulu shields, rifle, and spear" (ibid. 143). These images, then, are forms of speech acts that insist on appearing by and for the people, although they may be deemed lost or missing within the dominant framework.

The Till lynching may be considered the first in a seemingly running list of calls to witness the struggles of African Americans in the United States. Following the global spread of mobile media devices, images of the deaths of Michael Brown, Tamir Rice, Eric Garner, Sandra Bland, Philando Castille, Ahmaud Arbery, George Floyd and so many more have been added to the list. They continue to present the power to heal and provide a critical memory created through "a continuity in the development of black publicity rather than [] recurrent novelt[ies]" (Baker 1994,15). Critical memory is connected to the embodied experience of African Americans not only through the visceral act of witnessing physical struggle and death, but also through re-enactments and collective memory produced through expressive political culture actively preserving memory as an intellectual resource (Gilroy 1993, 39; see also Blaagaard 2018). Paul Gilroy takes care not to essentialise nor pluralise the cultural and political expressions of African Americans. Rather he emphasises the multiple connections and co-constructions of cultural and political meaning-making processes that extend the bounds of politics. In this way, crit-ical, collective memory expressed through images, texts, music and more produce the African American counter-public and counter-culture sustained through re-enactments and memory as well as political discourse and protests.

Today, the gate-keeper role of mass media – that prevented the image of Emmett Till from producing radical change – is diminished and social media images remind us all to bear witness from the perspective of the black community, in turn, intro-ducing the black gaze. bell hooks (2015, 115) theorises the gaze as "a gesture of resistance, challenge to authority", which gives opportunity to form an "enclaved" public sphere that functions as a safe space for preservation of minority voices although endowed with few resources to counter dominant discourse (Squires 2002, 457–459). Thus, choosing to stop looking may also be a gesture of resistance: "… turning away was one way to protest, to reject negation" producing an oppositional gaze that may allow for new representations to occur (hooks 2015, 212). However, introducing the black gaze and experience to white viewers potentially emerge as a political act and an act of political protest, which, in turn, produces a counter-public fostering resistance (Squires 2002, 460). The images that introduce the black gaze are simultaneously more than a simple recording and remembering of violations or perhaps a form of sousveillance. "[They are] an act of protest, too, since the black gaze has been outlawed historically" (Richardson 2018, 398). Traditionally, in the United States, enslaved African Americans were punished for returning the gaze of the overseer. Throughout the Jim Crow era and within the prison complex today, meeting a white person's gaze is done at the risk of punishment and death for a black person, argues Mirzoeff (2017, 88–89). Again, the embodied re-enactment of a gesture – in this case a gaze – produces a political and socio-historical rupture connecting memory to political protest.

The two modalities of oppositional publics – critical memory and political protest – intertwine and rely on each other. Catherine R. Squires (2002) differentiates between hidden resistance *enclaved* in safe spaces and *counter-publics* that draw heavily on embodied protests: sit-ins, demonstrations, boycotts etc.: "[i]f the enclave response is normally deployed in response to conditions of intense oppression, then counter-publics usually emerge in response to a decrease in oppression or an increase in resources" (Squires 2002, 460). Despite their obvious capitalist foundations and troubling lack of accountability, mobile media devices and social media have at times emerged to represent the current increase in resources as well as opportunities to engage critically in public discourse and returning the gaze. Adding to demonstrations, sit-ins and boycotts, the embodiedness of counter-publics is produced and performed through gestures and visual expressions, re-enacting the last words and final gestures of victims of police violence as they are fixed on the viral networks of social media. The gestures and the slogans – artifacts of engagement (Clark 2016) – prevail whether they are factual or not, Allissa V. Richardson (2018, 392) asserts "…because people need[] to shape chaotic events into a coherent story that [make] it easier to process". Shaping such events using the physical body, I argue in the remainder of this chapter, underscores the narrative and allows slogans and hashtags to be incorporated into flesh.

Artifacts of Engagements

I now turn to the discursive analysis of two cases of artifacts of engagement that followed the killings of Brown and Arbery. Artifacts of engagement to Lynn S. Clark (2016) are all interactions that are in play online and offline in protests. They are mediated responses and expressions "signaling political involvement" (235), thus making the approach highly appropriate to understand the double hashtags produced by the cases. Artifacts of engagement related to the killings help produce the visual counter-public of BLM (Clark 2016; Richardson 2016). BLM was founded in 2013 in response to the acquittal of Trayvon Martin's killer based on Florida's Stand Your Ground laws. While BLM Global Network Foundation Inc. represents the movement,[2] according to activist DeRay Mckesson, "it encompasses all who publicly declare that Black lives matter and devote their time and energy accordingly" (Freelon et al. 2016, 9). The movement fights white supremacy and has a special focus on the impunity of police violence against African Americans. In this way, the movement connects to previous civil rights issues in the United

States and the social and political work by the Black Panther Party, for instance, critiquing the prison complex (see Davis 2016/1971). The continuous killing of black people by the police and the ubiquitous presence of mobile and social media have produced viral imagery that, in turn, have produced protests and artifacts as well as continued support for the movement. The cases of "Hands up, don't shoot" and "#IRunWithMaud", which are used in this chapter, are part of these artifacts.

Because of the time frame presented by the case of Brown's killing, the empirical collection of artifactual expressions of "Hands up, don't shoot" is made in a purposive selection of artifacts on social media and legacy media. The purposive selection is produced through a visual discursive process "tracking how images, or versions of images – and their truth claims – move among different media and audiences" (Rose 2016, 195). The purpose of this approach is to allow me to refer to the widespread use of the gesture in a range of facets. In contrast, the data collected on the case of #IRunWithMaud is primarily based on the posts on the eponymous Facebook page[3] and Twitter[4] featuring images of people running 2.23 miles and dedicating their runs to Arbery. This selection is limited to the images disseminated and circulating in the spring of 2021.

The following analyses, then, are not based on particular images or posts, but on the gestures and processes of re-enactments themselves, which are understood as artifacts of engagements.

"Hands Up, Don't Shoot" and "#IRunWithMaud"

Following the killing of Brown, the words "Hands up, don't shoot" were displayed on placards at demonstrations against police violence. Moreover, the gesture of raising one's hands was enacted by protesters, politicians, football players and journalists alike in support of BLM's cause. The phrase and gesture were re-enactments of Brown's last words and gestures. Similarly, following the killing of Arbery the hashtag #IRunWithMaud was launched by supporters on what would have been his 26th birthday. Arbery was out running, when he was killed on 23 February 2020. Thus, a 2.23-mile run was organised to commemorate the date of his killing and participants and supporters following the initial run posted pictures on social media, showing their fitness tracking devices displaying 2.23 miles. In what follows, I identify discursive strands running through the gestures, hashtags, technologies and expressions of the two disparate artifacts of engagement, followed by a concluding discussion of their combined meaning-making powers as protest imagery on social media and production of counter-publics.

Vulnerability

In the autumn of 2014, the gesture of raising both hands in a sign of surrender, often accompanied by placards with the words "Hands up, don't shoot", became a rallying cry for and signal of support for BLM's cause. A student at Howard University, Washington D.C., captured and posted to social media a picture of his peers with raised hands filling the bleachers in the campus stadium, the gesture was seen at street protests captured by photojournalists, at football games as players entered the arena performing the gesture, in congressional settings and on news shows. Mimicking the last gesture and words of Michael Brown, the gesture travels as a re-enactment that presents the viewer with both the realisation of what immediately followed the moment when the gesture was performed by Brown and carries on that moment as an embodied commentary and standing accusation of the injustice his death represents.

Two discursive strands emerge from the re-enacted gesture of Brown: Firstly, and arguably, the gesture of raising one's hands could be perceived as a gesture of surrender and submission (Apel 2014), following, as it does, the narrative of white, reassuring publicity so prominent during the Civil Rights era (Berger 2011). This is not a missing image or an artifact of resistance and black agency. It is an artifact of injustice against a population that urges the spectators' empathy and action. This argument is supported by the co-optation of the gesture in white communities of power, such as the journalists at CNN's Newsroom programme.[5] The ease with which the gesture is re-enacted by a roundtable of three white women and one woman of colour speaks to its absorbability. The gesture provides a safe narrative of "performed reassuring symbolic work" (Berger 2011, 6) within which the white audience may see themselves as allies. Secondly, however, the frozen state of Brown's death continually re-enacted and called into memory reminds the viewers of the particular and structural vulnerability of African American existence. "The body implies mortality, vulnerability, agency", writes Judith Butler (2009, 26). Flaunting bodily vulnerability by posing in a way that exposes the neck and chest and limits opportunity of self-defence, the embodied gesture of "Hands up, don't shoot" creates the constant memory of Brown's vulnerable, dying body. Kate Drazner Hoyt (2016, 31) refers to this performance as transforming the slogan "from a space for standing *with* [Brown] to a state of standing *within* the body in peril". The gesture disrupts the desired closure enabling societies to forget and move on from trauma and tragedy to action. It places Brown's dead body among the living, because it is inhabited by the protester and performers, and thereby breaks down closure. "Remembering", argues Ann Fabian (2010, 60) on the dead and visible bodies left by Hurricane Katrina, "can be a forensic exercise, not to learn about the identity of the dead or why they died, but a forensic exercise to learn something about those of us who looked at Katrina's dead". The vulnerability of the dead points to the myth of American self-sufficiency by showing, in contrast, the interdependencies of living bodies and subjects. The re-enacted gesture of Brown – "standing *within* [his] body in peril" (Hoyt 2016, 31) – makes visible the continued social struggle and the societal structures that necessitate the struggle. The gesture insists that Brown's life is grievable and grief becomes a catalyst for political action (Butler 2009, 22; Fabian 2010, 66).

Although differing in subtext, both discourses are simultaneously possible, because the gesture functions as an embodied version of the digital hashtag thereby producing a *double hashtag*. Hashtags are "connective affordances [that] invite forms of expressions and connection that frequently help liberate the individual and collective imaginations" (Papacharissi 2016, 310). In her influential writings on affective publics, Zizi Papacharissi shows how hashtags produce affective discourses that "identify[] publics and counter publics, and thus discursively render[] publics within and beyond or against the tag articulations" (ibid. 315). Like hashtags, physical gestures are emotive and phatic and enable a sense of connectivity within counter-publics. They are moreover ordering processes that produce a structure to chaotic feelings. This is why, argues Richardson (2018, 392), they are necessary in order to make sense of distressing times and events. However, hashtags may also run the risk of platformisation and marketisation of the vulnerable (Chouliaraki 2021). Lilie Chouliaraki argues:

> Claims to suffering, delinked from those who are subjected to the multiple harms of neoliberalism and attached to those who most benefit from it, … [may] … ultimately obfuscate the structural conditions of the most vulnerable and avoid restoring the harms done or addressing the injustices that cause it.
>
> *2021, 22*

By presenting the possibility of co-optation and abuse of the political message of vulnerability, this argument goes beyond the risk of performing reassuring symbolic work. Whether "Hands up, don't shoot" is risking the clarity and importance of the political message or works as a catalyst for political action, the gesture convenes around "logic of affective communication" or "affective commonalities" (Chouliaraki 2021, 20; Papacharissi 2016, 318) that may potentially enable political or social re-imaginings.

Endurance

If "Hands up, don't shoot" is an artifact of engagement that was deployed throughout multiple media and political spheres, #IRunWithMaud and the re-enacted embodiment of Arbery's last gesture exists mainly online on sites such as Twitter and Facebook. While "Hands up, don't shoot" was performed by individuals as well as crowds, #IRunWithMaud was mainly an individual affair. Although collective runs were organised, they were performed individually due to the Covid-19 pandemic, which made gatherings in large crowds risky after March 2020. Thus, celebrities, athletes and other individuals made their runs for Arbery public through social media and often by posting evidence of their exercise by showing images of their tracking devices. The 2.23 miles run was launched by Arbery's friends and family on his birthday on 8 May and continues to be performed as of the time of writing.[6] The gesture, then, simultaneously commemorates his date of birth and the date of his death and beyond. In this way, the gesture insists on presenting the viewer with the knowledge of Arbery's life, rather than focusing exclusively on his untimely and unjust death.

#IRunWithMaud underscores the insistence on the importance of Arbery's life as well as the implications of his death by reproducing the gesture of running 2.23 miles. Running is a life-enhancing and life-extending exercise that emphasises Arbery's fitness for life. Re-enacting the exercise, re-enacts his potential for and in life. Running moreover requires physical endurance. The discourse developed by means of the hashtag, then, is one of vitality and the endurance and continuation of life. In her 2013 book, *The Posthuman*, Rosi Braidotti proposes a different way of dealing with the reality of violence and destruction (Braidotti 2013, 122). Rather than focusing on the human condition as one directed towards and delimited by death, Braidotti argues for "the construction of affirmative alternatives" (ibid. 130) that entails a relational ethics that goes beyond the individual's life and death situation and produces a continued transformative becoming – that is, *zoe*, which "carries on, relentlessly" (ibid. 131). Endurance, then, is to be understood in its double form of "temporal duration or continuity and spatial suffering or sustainability" (ibid. 132). #IRunWithMaud, arguably, produces a figuration of complex responses to the unjustifiable violence against African Americans. The figuration is recognised in the lost images of critical memory of black agency and resistance that similarly underscore the endurance and sustainability of resistance (Berger 2011; Baker 1994). Focusing on the endurance of Arbery's potential for life, the gesture of running 2.23 miles in his honour underscores the continuation of resistance and struggle, despite the suffering it inflicts.

The double hashtag – the digital and the embodied – provide a connective action (Bennett and Segerberg 2012) with a twist, because one does not make much sense without the other. While the gesture of raising one's hands in surrender is recognisable to most, running 2.23 miles is less familiar in the context of activism. #IRunWithMaud may be construed as a connective action network, which is "individualized and technologically organized [without the] requirement of collective identity framing" (ibid. 750). On Facebook and Twitter, the solidarity runners are diverse in age, ethnicity, geographical locations and genders motivated by the injustice they have witnessed via social media. Behind the hashtag, however, is the grassroot law project *Justice for Ahmaud*[7] and change.org petitions,[8] among others. Of course, BLM understood as a kind of umbrella organisation fighting for justice and a reformed police and prison system may also be seen as organisationally enabling the online connective action network, which would put #IRunWithMaud in Lance W. Bennett and Alexandra Segerberg's category of "connective action organizationally enabled networks" (756). However, more interesting to the argument made in this chapter is the use of the embodied hashtag or gesture that – like in the case of "Hands up, don't shoot" – presents as phatic and emotive generating connective sentiments (Papacharissi 2016). #IRunWithMaud is accompanied by the physical act of running 2.23 miles proving the endurance of resistance. Sharing one's own support alongside many others' produces an imagined community, which may not amount to connectivity, but which certainly calls on a common understanding or relational ethics.

The artifact, moreover, generates critical memory as an intellectual resource. As an example, I may present the TikTok account @elliethegreathonorablem, who has continued to run every day since the death of Arbery. Each day he posts a short video of his run accompanied by the text "I will run everyday [sic] until Ahmaud Arbery gets justice".[9] The sustained run and posts suggest an embodied memory that performs a legal rights claim. The run is a resistance of endurance, because @elliethegreathonorablem enacts the body and subjectivity of Arbery by repeating his movements. But it is moreover an entry in the continued critical memory of African American lives, which brings the understanding that everyday chores and exercises are potentially lethal. @elliethegreathonorablem insists on continuing to run while black – the everyday situation that cost Arbery his life.

Concluding Discussion

The analyses above show that rather than appropriations of iconic imagery reproducing an abstract white public, the gestural character of both "Hands up, don't shoot" and "#IRunWithMaud" appropriate embodied political acts that challenge iconicity's embedded whiteness (Blaagaard 2019, 255). This is accomplished by engaging in critical memory (Baker 1994) and producing a space of appearance. The space of appearance is an embodied and political space, created through visuality *for* and *by* the people and is not only *about* them, claims Mirzoeff (2017). Professional photojournalism may produce both empathic and political images, but will never, according to Mirzoeff, invoke a space of appearance (Ibid., 40). The artifacts of engagement analysed in this chapter, however, achieve this political act of producing a space of appearance by introducing the black gaze embodied in experience and thereby creating a counter-public and counter-culture (Gilroy 1993). The artifacts go beyond the limits of textuality and produce a double hashtag – one digital, the other embodied – while creating an affective public (Papacharissi 2016). While protests using social media continue to run the risk of "delink[ing] from those who are subjected to the multiple harms of neoliberalism" (Chouliaraki 2021, 22) and racism, the insistence on re-enacting and embodying the hashtag, which "Hands up, don't shoot" and "#IRunWithMaud" perform, potentially transpose digital connectivity into something akin to embodied collectivity.

However, the transposition is not a monolith. A counter-public based on the discourse of vulnerability in the current political climate may prompt counterclaims and co-optations. Vulnerability, Chouliaraki argues, runs the risk of turning into victimhood, that is, "an act of affective communication that attaches the moral value accrued to the vulnerable to everyone who claims it" (Chouliaraki 2021, 12). Victimhood is constructed in current political discourse, for instance, through the slogan "white lives matter" or "blue lives matter" in response to the vulnerability of African American lives. Because victimhood detaches the claimant from the actual vulnerability of their condition, it lacks substance and accountability. For this reason, social media protests focusing on vulnerability need to be based on the distinction between claim and condition incorporating questions of position and power (Chouliaraki 2021, 22), that is, questions of grievable lives (Butler 2009). On a different set, a counter-public created through discourses of endurance rejects victimhood in favour of a focus on sustained and sustaining relational ethics of life or *zoe*. This, however, does not mean that the discourse of endurance is safe from co-optation or abuse. The risk consists of deflating and devaluing the loss of life commemorated through the double hashtag, making it into yet another consumer product.

The predicaments of the double hashtags discussed in this chapter show their implications and importance to political discourse and protests on social media. On the one hand, the digital quality of the gestural protest imagery makes affective publics and connective action possible. On the other hand, the embodied quality of the artifacts of engagement allows an emphasis on the conditions of the claimant to suffering or vulnerability, thereby supporting the lived experience and critical memory. In combination, they potentially and slowly challenge iconic protest imagery and, following, the way societies are viewed, how publics are performed and how history is told.

Notes

1 Stand Your Ground laws are widespread across the United States and allow citizens to defend themselves anywhere and with deadly force if they feel threatened.
2 https://blacklivesmatter.com/about/ accessed July 18, 2021.
3 www.facebook.com/hashtag/irunwithmaud accessed April 26, 2021.
4 https://twitter.com/hashtag/irunwithmaud accessed April 26, 2021.
5 www.youtube.com/watch?v=ha1ljAbOPnY accessed April 26, 2021.
6 See for instance: www.dailydot.com/unclick/ahmaud-arbery-tiktok-running-every-day/ ?Fb=dd&fbclid=IwAR2h6v1hgsJKNJ-egiUW-g6r61jypVY5I-S6uuIChXR49dOPWtpl ZoDRa4E accessed April 26, 2021.
7 www.runwithmaud.com/ accessed April 26, 2021.
8 www.change.org/p/glynn-county-distric-attorney-justice-for-ahmaud-arbery accessed April 26, 2021.
9 See footnote 4.

Bibliography

Apel, D. 2014. "'Hands up, don't shoot' surrendering to liberal illusions." *Theory & Event* 17, no. 3.
Baker, H. 1994. "Critical memory and the black public sphere." *Public Culture* 7, no. 1: 3–33.
Bennett, W. L. and A. Segerberg. 2012. "The logic of connective action." *Information, Communication & Society* 15, no. 5:739–768.
Berger, M. A. 2011. *Seeing through race: A reinterpretation of civil rights photography*. Berkeley and London: University of California Press.
Blaagaard, B. B. 2018. "Rosi Braidotti and Paul Gilroy: Questions of memory and cosmopolitan futures of Europe". In *Postcolonial intellectuals in Europe: Critics, artists, movements, and their publics*, edited by S. Ponzanesi and A. J. Habed, 123–139. London and New York: Rowman & Littlefield.

Blaagaard, B. B. 2019. "Picturing the political: Embodied visuality of protest imagery." In *Visual political communication*, edited by A. Veneti, D. Jackson, and D. G. Lilleker, 247–264. London: Palgrave MacMillan.

Blaagaard, B. B., M. Mortensen, and C. Neumayer. 2017. "Digital images, globalized conflict." *Media, Culture & Society* 39, no. 8: 1111–1121.

Blaagaard, B. B. and M. M. Roslyng. 2020. "The spatial, networked, and embodied agency of social media: A critical discourse perspective on Banksy's political expression. *Critical discourse studies*, E-pub ahead of print.

Braidotti, R. 2013. *The posthuman*. Cambridge: Polity.

Butler, J. 2009. *Precarious life*. New York and London: Verso Books.

Clark, L. S. 2016. "Participants on the margins: #BlackLivesMatter and the role that shared artifacts of engagement played among minoritized political newcomers on Snapchat, Facebook, and Twitter." *International Journal of Communication* 10, no. 26: 235–253.

Chouliaraki, L. 2021. "Victimhood: the affective politics of vulnerability." *European Journal of Cultural Studies* 24, no. 1: 10–27.

Chouliaraki, L. and T. Stolic. 2017. "Rethinking media responsibility in the refugee 'crisis': a visual typology of European news." *Media, Culture & Society* 39, no. 8: 1162–1177.

Davis, A. Y. 2016/1971. "Political prisoners, prisons and black liberation". In *They come in the morning … voices of resistance*, edited by A. Y. Davis, 27–43. London and New York: Verso Books.

Fabian, A. 2010. "Seeing Katrina's dead." In *Katrina's imprint: Race and vulnerability in America*, edited by R. Anglin, 59–68. New Brunswick: Rutgers University Press.

Fraser, N. 1991. "Rethinking the public sphere: A contribution to the critique of actually existing democracy." In *Habermas and the public sphere*, edited by C. Calhoun, 56–80. Cambridge: MIT Press.

Freelon, D., C. D. McIlwain, and M. D. Clark. 2016. *Beyond the hashtags*. Washington D.C.: Center for Media and Social Impacts. Available online: https://cmsimpact.org/wp-content/uploads/2016/03/beyond_the_hashtags_2016.pdf

Gilroy, P. 1993. *The Black Atlantic*. London and New York: Verso Books.

Habermas, J. 1989. *The structural transformation of the public sphere*. Translated by T. Burger. Cambridge: MIT Press.

Hariman, R. and J. L. Lucaites. 2007. *No caption needed: Iconic photographs, public culture, and liberal democracy*. Chicago and London: University of Chicago Press.

hooks, bell. 2015. "The oppositional gaze: Black female spectators". In *Black looks: Race and representation*, 115–132. New York: Routledge.

Hoyt, K. D. 2016. "The affect of the hashtag: #Handsupdontshoot and the body in peril." *Explorations in Media Ecology* 15, no. 1: 29–50.

Isin, E. and G. Nielsen. (eds.). 2008. *Acts of citizenship*. London and New York: Zed Books.

Mirzoeff, N. 2011. *The Right to Look. A counterhistory of visuality*. Durham: Duke University Press.

Mirzoeff, N. 2017. *The appearance of Black lives matter*. Miami: Name Publication.

Papacharissi, Z. 2016. "Affective publics and structures of storytelling: Sentiments, events and mediality." *Information, Communication & Society* 19, no. 3: 307–324.

Richardson, A. V. 2016. "Bearing witness while Black: Theorizing African American mobile journalism after Ferguson." *Digital Journalism* 5, no. 6: 673–698.

Richardson, A. V. 2018. "A phenomenology of black lives matter journalist- activists". In *The Routledge handbook of developments in digital journalism studies*, edited by S. Eldridge II and B. Franklin, 387–400. Abingdon: Routledge.

Rose, G. 2016. *Visual methodologies* (4th ed.). London: Sage.

Squires, C. R. 2002. "Rethinking the Black public sphere: An alternative vocabulary for multiple public Spheres." *Communication Theory*, 12, no. 4: 446–468.

Warner, M. 1992. "The mass public and the mass subject." In *Habermas and the public sphere*, edited by C. Calhoun, 377–401. Cambridge: MIT Press.

Warner, M. 2002. "Publics and counter-publics." *Public Culture* 14, no. 1: 49–90.

6
IMAGE CENSORSHIP ON CHINESE SOCIAL MEDIA

Image Deletion on Weibo during the 2014 Hong Kong Umbrella Movement

Jun Liu

While earlier scholarship has claimed the Internet as a free, independent space beyond state and commercial intervention, nowadays scholars increasingly acknowledge that online content moderation – or censorship in short – is becoming more complex and agile, thanks to technological advancements (e.g. Dick 2012; Deibert et al. 2011; Deibert and Rohozinski 2010; Roberts 2019; Keremoğlu and Weidmann 2020). Reportedly, two-thirds of Internet users still live with some types of online censorship (AFP and Beall 2016). Among studies that investigate Internet censorship in different contexts (e.g. Casilli and Tubaro 2012; Aceto and Pescapé 2015; Deibert et al. 2008; Keremoğlu and Weidmann 2020), China's Internet censorship, described as "the most extensive, technologically sophisticated, and broad-reaching system of Internet filtering in the world" (Opennet Initiative 2005, 4), has drawn extensive attention from academia and wider society. The online censorship system employs vast networks of thousands of workers and automated filtering software to track down problematic content and alleged miscreants among the country's 800 million Internet users (e.g. King et al. 2013, 2014, 2017).

Although studies have generated rich and nuanced understandings of online censorship in China, most of them have an exclusive focus on textual content removal. Subsequently, less is known about how online censorship mechanism removes posts containing "politically sensitive" meanings conveyed in non-textual or multimedia forms (however, see Liu and Zhao 2021). Furthermore, which criteria does a censorship mechanism adopt when it filters out multimedia online content? To answer these questions, this chapter presents one of the first studies on possible criteria regarding multimedia censorship, with a particular focus on image removal. The discussion offers theoretical insights and pragmatic implications for understanding online multimedia censorship during conflicts, which is an understudied topic in current censorship scholarship. More specifically, for one thing, image censorship involves not only automated image recognition technologies,

DOI: 10.4324/9781003176923-7

but also significant manual effort to ensure the inclusion of politically sensitive multimedia content regarding conflict in question. For another, the image removal strategy demonstrates a deliberate manipulation by an authoritarian regime to distract people from visual content about conflict and collective mobilisation, given the consideration that these contents entail greater attention-capturing capacity and a longer lifespan and thus potentially a larger influence compared to textual content.

In the sections below, this chapter first presents a review of scholarship on Chinese Internet censorship. While acknowledging scholars' contributions, this study pinpoints and addresses an existing gap: that of censorship which targets multimedia messaging (i.e. not only that which contains text but imagery, as well). Second, the chapter explicates the theoretical reasoning and hypotheses. Third, it lays out the methodology, including case selection, data collection and data analysis. Finally, the chapter presents the findings and discussions with plausible explanations, limitations and concluding reflections.

Internet Censorship in China: A Critical Review

Despite its substantial contribution, existing censorship scholarship has predominantly focused on text (removal), failing to account for multimedia censorship, which subsequently presents an incomplete, or distorted picture of the sophistication of censorship mechanisms. More specifically, earlier scholarship largely addresses macro-level policy, legal and technological aspects of Internet censorship. While this chapter is not intended to provide a comprehensive overview of existing censorship literature, its focus is on the mechanism of Internet censorship in China as a crucial topic especially in recent years (e.g. Fu et al. 2013; King et al. 2013, 2014; Knockel et al. 2018; Qin et al. 2017).

Past research has investigated regime policy and the policing of the Internet in China, including regulatory control (MacKinnon 2008; Liang and Lu 2010; Pan 2017; Esarey and Kluver 2014), as well as the technical infrastructure of the "Great Firewall of China" (Barme and Ye 1997), such as techniques of filtering, domain name system poisoning and virtual private network blocking (Xu et al. 2011; Farnan et al. 2016; Deibert et al. 2008; Sfakianakis et al. 2011). In recent years, the emergence and increasing adoption of digitally aided techniques allow scholars to harvest large-scale data sets – unavailable earlier due to the lack or the difficulty of access – and to depict nuanced pictures of how a censorship programme is implemented (e.g. Bamman et al. 2012; Fu et al. 2013; King et al. 2013, 2014; Knockel et al. 2018; Qin et al. 2017, Zhu et al. 2013). Observation and scrutiny of politically driven censorship deletion practices with computational methods better illuminate notoriously elusive, obscure and fickle censorship patterns that are "far more nuanced than a simple blacklist" (Bamman et al. 2012).

More specifically, studies on the censorship of the Chinese Internet reveal deletion mechanisms in terms of content-based, geographical and temporal preferences. King and his colleagues' (2013, 2014, 2017) serial studies on Chinese social media censorship offer one of the most extensive interrogations of content preference for censorship deletion. With an estimated rate of approximately 13% censorship, this type of deletion principally targets textual content with offline collective action mobilisation potential, regardless of the authors' support or criticism of the government. With 13.2 billion posts which are publicly available on Sina Weibo (hereafter "Weibo"), Qin et al. (2017) discover "millions of posts on Sina Weibo that discuss sensitive collective action events", (p. 127), indicating that the regime tolerates "even the most sensitive collective action events", so far as they do not pose a threat. In other words, censorship involves removing content about "large regime-threatening protests" (Qin et al. 2017, 138). Bamman et al. (2012) reveal a geographical preference for deletion: "messages originating in the outlying provinces … [exhibit] much higher deletion rates than those from eastern areas" due to attention to sensitive areas such as Tibet. Through a timing analysis of 2.38 million Weibo posts, Zhu et al. (2013) illustrate a temporal preference by demonstrating that 90% of the deletion happens within the first 24 hours.

Without denying the significant contribution from extant scholarship, it remains dominated by an exclusive focus on the textual content removal phenomenon on the Internet, as Liu and Zhao (2021) point out. In other words, the vast majority of censorship literature has been concerned with textual elements in online posts – and consequently a *textual*-based censorship mechanism only. Nevertheless, in actuality, censorship is rarely only automated and often consists of manual deletion based on text (Bamman et al. 2012; Fu et al. 2013; King et al. 2013; Zhu et al. 2013; Qin et al. 2017). Zhu et al. (2013, 230) show that three out of four deleted social media posts involve pictures, yet the reason behind such a deletion phenomenon remains unclear. Dou (2017) also argues that, in some cases, text-based interaction remains "largely unaffected", while messages with photo and video suffer "disruptions". Similarly, the summary that King et al. (2013, 328) make, "content filtering is in large part a manual effort – censors read post by hand", implies that censors also target non-textual or multimedia content. Most importantly, although studies claim that posting multimedia images about politically sensitive issues is an effective way to evade censorship (e.g. Mina 2014), Liu and Zhao's study (2021) demonstrates that multimedia posts suffered more intensive censorship deletion than plain-text posts, with the censorship programme directed more towards multimedia content like images than the text content of multimedia posts. Despite these efforts, limited insight exists regarding multimedia censorship, leaving this topic fundamentally understudied. For instance, while Liu and Zhao (2021) advance one of the first studies to encapsulate a preference for multimedia posts over plain text regarding censorship online in China, their study only offers a general overview, rather than probing the censorship criteria mechanism that may be adopted when it filters out online multimedia content.

Censoring Image Posts: Theories and Hypotheses

To fill the gap, this study takes a further step to explore plausible criteria that shape censorship mechanisms against multimedia content, with a specific focus on imagery. Censorship in this study refers to content deletion, rather than "content blocking" (Pan 2017, 168), "search censorship" (Bamman et al. 2012) or information flooding (Roberts 2018, 5). Historically speaking, in the beginning, censorship primarily targeted the written word (Patterson 1993; Jansen 1988). Censorship later extended to non-textual communication, such as musical recordings, television, film (Biltereyst et al. 2013; Müller 2004) and particularly images (Freedberg 1989; Allison 2000). These media attracted censors' attention, as they reveal more than what is allowed to be shown (Gilbert 2013) and attain greater social reach with a more immediate and cumulative impact than the written word (Biltereyst et al. 2013; Coetzee 2018). Subsequently, they proved difficult for authorities to control (e.g. Couvares 2006). In particular, scholarship dedicated to visuals during war and conflicts concluded that the immediacy, ease of distribution and memorable qualities of the images led to greater emotional response, quicker dissemination and consequently a higher impact in comparison with textual ones (e.g. Hansen 2011; Schwalbe and Dougherty 2015; Makhortykh and Sydorova 2017). Such "powerful and potentially persuasive information about the people, places, and events that they [the images] represent" has drawn "aggressive censorship" (English 2012, 106, 121) of controlling especially images of conflicts such as war and violence throughout history (e.g. Friis 2015; Hutchinson 1985).

To complement existing scholarship that largely does not cover the censorship of images, this chapter considers studies of image recognition as well as a some on the censorship of multimedia content on the Chinese social media platform Weibo (e.g. Zhao et al. 2013), and other platforms like WeChat. The justification of case selection will be presented in the next section. While no study examines image censorship on Weibo, Knockel et al. (2018) discover a visual-based image algorithm that identifies "images that are visually similar to those on an image blacklist". The algorithm is similar to what studies elsewhere acknowledge about image content recognition, including colour- and shape-related information and local feature descriptors. Similar techniques have been adopted by Facebook and Twitter, for instance, to identify obscene, pornographic or sexually explicit images (Ries and Lienhart 2014; Bhoyar and Kakde 2010). In a similar vein, this study proposes that Weibo employs an image recognition technology that pinpoints posts containing the imagery part with recognisable elements for censorship deletion consideration. By "recognisable elements", this study denotes specific perceptible colour- or shape-related descriptors of an image. Accordingly, this study suggests the first hypothesis as:

> *Hypothesis 1 (H1): Multimedia posts with images containing recognisable elements suffer a higher level of censorship deletion than those without these elements.*

Furthermore, despite the limited amount of research on multimedia, and specifically, image, censorship, established studies have shed some light on possible criteria. King et al.'s (2013, 333) seminal study demonstrates that social media content with the potential to stimulate collective action, is "considerably more censored" than other content. More specifically, as King et al. (2013, 335) illustrate, "posts related to collective action events will be censored regardless of whether they criticise the state, with both critical and supportive posts uncensored when events have no collective action potential". Furthermore, given that "the censors are highly accurate and aimed at increasing censorship magnitude", King et al. (2013, 328, 334) propose that "content filtering is in large part a manual effort", as "[a]utomated methods of individual classification are not capable of this high a level of accuracy". Following King et al.'s argument, this study poses a similar hypothesis regarding the analysis of image censorship on Chinese social media:

> *Hypothesis 2 (H2): Multimedia posts with images containing collective action potential, regardless of whether they are supportive of the state, or otherwise, suffer a higher level of censorship deletion than posts without such content.*

Methods

Case Selection

In referencing "social media", this study specifically examines the censorship deletion in Weibo, one of the most popular social media channels in China's (for general discussions on Weibo, see Sullivan 2012, 2014). Weibo has been chosen for the following reason: with its 431 million monthly active users in June 2018 (China Internet Watch Team 2018), Weibo maintains an influential platform in contemporary China. Over 130 million daily active users have maintained Weibo as a vibrant, contested and high-visibility space in which people express and share opinions on political issues, disclose and criticise government malfeasance and mobilise and coordinate political action even "before authorities and censors c[an] react" (Chan et al. 2012, 348). Furthermore, while WeChat is primarily for private chatting and sharing among close circles of friends, Weibo is "much more open and public" (Yu and Xu 2016, 83), as anyone on Weibo can view almost anyone else's posts and retweet them. This highly interactive environment with a low threshold of participation encourages posts on Weibo to spread rapidly and topics to quickly peak or "trend" thus receiving large-scale attention (e.g. Huang and Sun 2014; Yu et al. 2015). For this reason, the authorities are struggling to keep Weibo under effective control (Bamman et al. 2012; Fu et al. 2013; Zhu et al. 2013; Moore 2012). Hence Weibo has become a prime example of a platform that suffers from intensive regulation, recurrent crackdown and extensive censorship.

To study image censorship on Weibo, this study chose the case of the Umbrella Movement (hereafter "UM") in Hong Kong in 2014, also known as "the Occupy Central movement". The UM was a political action that lasted from September until December 2014. The protestors were demanding the realisation of genuine universal suffrage, the resignation of then Chief Executive Leung Chun-Ying, the withdrawal of the National People's Congress Standing Committee's decision to preselect candidates for the 2017 Chief Executive elections and the submission of a new electoral reform plan (for details, see Albert 2016). Both government officials in Hong Kong and in Beijing, including the official media, denounced the movement as "illegal" and a "violation of the rule of law" (*People's Daily's* commentary writer 2014, Staff Writer 2018).

Even though the confrontation happened outside the Chinese mainland, it did attract general attention among Internet users in mainland China. This popularity made terms like "Hong Kong" and "Occupy Central" trending topics on Weibo (Kuo 2014). *The China Society Yearbook (Shehui Lan Pi shui)*, published by an official think tank called the Chinese Academy of Social Sciences, which discusses social issues and changes in the previous year, ranked UM as the second of the top 20 high-profile topics among Chinese Internet users (Sing Pao 2015). Chinese government authorities issued a censorship directive on 28 September 2014 that demanded immediate deletion of "information about Hong Kong students violently assaulting the government and about 'Occupy Central'. … Strictly manage interactive channels, and resolutely delete harmful information" (Rudolph 2014). Furthermore, in King et al.'s (2014, 1251722) study, they observe that "there is no censorship of posts about collective action events outside mainland China". The UM case is, nevertheless, apparently a "deviant" case (Seawright and Gerring 2008), with a recorded degree of censorship, particularly aimed at images, as reported by Liu and Zhao (2021) and the Weiboscope (http://weiboscope.jmsc.hku.hk/), a censorship monitoring project at the University of Hong Kong (HKU) (Boehler 2014). Subsequently, the UM has become a relevant but understudied case for scrutinising censorship in Weibo.

Data Collection and Analysis

To answer our two hypotheses, this study collected and compared *both* censored and accessible Weibo posts which have survived openly and which are related to the UM. It focused on posts from a relatively modest number of Weibo users, monitored by Weiboscope, who are essentially either dissidents or "Weibo celebrities" with large social influence, given their large number of followers (Fu et al. 2013).

Immediately after the UM, data were collected through several steps. First, this study collected two months' period of censored posts between September 28 (the date that the Beijing government issued the censorship directive) and November 28 (the date that HK authorities took assertive action to demolish protests camps with support for the occupation declining (BBC 2014) from Weiboscope' social media timeline on Twitter (Fu et al. 2013). Data between October 12 and 20 were missing due to a hardware failure of the data collection server. Disregarding the two posts between October 12 and 20, Weiboscope recorded 2,336 censored posts in total (from 1,382 accounts), among which there were 1,195 censored posts relating to the UM (51.2%, from 712 Weibo accounts). Censored posts on other topics numbered 1,141 (48.8%). We randomly selected 120 posts, or 10% of the total censored posts, as the "censored data set".

Second, this study harvested all publicly available posts from the 712 accounts that posted the UM-related information but got deleted during the two months period via the User Timeline API function. A total of 93,477 posts were collected. The removal of the posts between October 12 and October 20 resulted in 81,762 posts, which, among other topics, involved posts about the UM but were not censored. As this study was only interested in posts related to the UM, I first took a random sample of 10% of the 81,762 posts (i.e. 8,176 posts) and then manually identified those about the UM (but survived censorship deletion), which turned out to be 564 posts as the "surviving data set".

Finally, this study created a coding scheme using an iterative process with visual content analysis (Bell 2011) to reflect (1) the post's elements, namely only plain text, image or long Weibo (a text-into-image conversion that turns posts of up to 10,000 characters into image files that can be shown using zoom in/out and rotation functions), a combination of plain text and image, long Weibo or URL, a combination of image and URL, image and long Weibo, long Weibo and URL, or plain text, image, long Weibo, and URL, or others (e.g. URL-only or video), (2) whether the imagery part contained recognisable elements and (3) a narrative of the imagery part with regards to collective action potential. Visual framing analysis (Schwalbe et al. 2008, Geise 2017), or framing analysis for visual images, was adopted particularly to interrogate the narrative of the imagery part. Following Entman's definition, framing denotes a process "to select some aspects of a perceived reality and make them more salient" (1993, 52) to the audience. While most framing analyses address textual content, Messaris and Abraham (2001, 220) propose that the special qualities of visuals allow the use of images to be especially effective for "framing and articulating ideological messages". Given such discussion, this study focused on whether the images entailed positive (i.e. expressing a supporting sentiment), negative (i.e. expressing a negative attitude) or neutral (stating a fact, such as news coverage) attitudes to collective action participation, or "unclear" messages (for ambiguous cases). Posts with collective action potential involve those containing images with either supportive or negative attitude towards collective action mobilisation. Codings were produced by two independent coders familiar with Chinese social media and politics, each of whom applied the set of codes to all images in both censored and surviving datasets. Intercoder reliability, measured by Cohen's kappa, was between 0.731 and 0.807. In short, a mixed method design in this study furthers methodological approaches to visual media by both providing rarely available, innovative datasets regarding image deletion and advancing an in-depth information and knowledge of the deletion.

Findings and Discussion

Hypothesis Testing

In the censored data set (n = 120), one post could not be displayed for an unknown reason (see Table 6.1). Among the remaining posts (n = 119), 109 posts contained both textual and imagery elements, five had image-only, four had text and long Weibo and one had "others" (e.g. URLs). The censored data set did not have plain

TABLE 6.1 Results of Distributions and Chi-Square Tests of Censored and Surviving Posts with Different Elements

Post Characteristics		Censored		Surviving		χ^2
		Exp. Freq.	Obs. Freq.	Exp. Freq.	Obs. Freq.	
Plain text		31.3	0 (0%)	146.7	178 (100.0%)	50.911★★★
Multimedia post		88.7	119 (23.6%)	416.3	385 (76.4%)	
Posts with images involving recognisable elements	Yes	15.7	26 (40.0%)	49.3	39 (60.0%)	10.309★★
	No	99.3	89 (21.7%)	311.7	322 (78.3%)	
Narrative of the image regarding collective action mobilisation	Positive	23.9	47 (47.5%)	75.1	52 (52.5%)	87.088★★★
	Negative	27.3	46 (40.7%)	85.7	67 (59.3%)	
	Neutral	36.2	5 (3.3%)	113.8	145 (96.7%)	
	Unclear	27.5	17 (14.9%)	86.5	97 (85.1%)	

★★★$p < .001$
★★$p < .01$

text post but were *all* multimedia posts. In the surviving data set (valid n = 563, one invalid with undisplayable content), 357 posts, contained both textual and imagery elements, 178 posts were plain text, 17 had both text and long Weibo, 10 were image-only and one belonged to "others". Multimedia posts (n = 385) comprised 68.4% of the total number of posts in the surviving data set.

To test the hypotheses, we further removed posts including only emojis among those with elements of imagery (i.e. posts with both textual and imagery elements or posts which were image-only) in both data sets. The removal left 476 posts in total, with 114 in the censored data set and 362 in the surviving data set. More specifically, in the censored data set, of the total 114 multimedia posts containing imagery, the number of those containing an image with an identified element was 21.9% (n = 25), while those without an identified element was 78.1% (n = 89). In the surviving data set, of the total 362 multimedia posts containing imagery, posts with an identified element constituted 10.8% (n = 39), while those without the element was 89.2% (n = 323).

H1 states that posts with imagery containing recognisable elements suffer a higher level of censorship deletion compared to those without these elements. To test this hypothesis, the study used the distributions of censored and surviving posts with images involving recognisable elements and ran a χ^2 test. The analysis revealed that the posts of the censored and the surviving groups were not equally distributed, with the observed proportion of censored posts with images involving recognisable elements being significantly higher than expected, χ^2 (1, N = 476) = 10.309, $p < .01$ (Table 6.1). The observed proportion of censored posts with images involving recognisable elements was significantly lower than expected. For instance, multimedia posts with images, or memes, containing the umbrella, politicians Leung Chun-ying, Hong Kong's then chief executive, and Carrie Lam Cheng Yuet-ngor, then Chief Secretary for Administration, and activist Chow Yong Kang Alex were deleted, notwithstanding their mobilisation-initiative-free contents. This finding confirms *H1*, as censorship deletion has a significantly higher deletion rate regarding posts with images involving recognisable elements.

H2 hypothesises that posts with collective action mobilisation potential suffer a higher level of censorship deletion than those without such potential. We use the distributions of posts containing images with different attitudes towards collective action mobilisation in both censored and surviving data sets to run a χ^2 test (Table 6.1). The analysis shows that the observed proportion of posts containing images with *both* positive and negative attitudes towards collective action mobilisation in the censored data set was significantly higher than expected, χ^2 (1, N = 476) = 87.088, $p < .001$. Furthermore, multimedia posts with narratives that either support mobilisation or oppose mobilisation have been removed, regardless of even the latter one involving information from the administrative agency of the State Council in Hong Kong, that is, the Hong Kong and Macao Affairs Office. The finding hereby confirms *H2*, as censorship deletion has a significantly higher deletion rate towards posts involving images with collective action mobilisation potential, *regardless* of whether the narratives of the images support or oppose mobilisation.

Theoretical and Pragmatical Implications

There are two plausible explanations for censorship deletion observed in this study. For one thing, as a further study based on Liu and Zhao (2021) this analysis offers a preliminary confirmation of the deployment of image recognition technology to detect the politically sensitive, recognisable imagery element in social media. As illustrated, imagery elements such as the iconic image of the umbrella or those of prominent politician and activists have been identified and subsequently integrated into a content removal mechanism. While it remains difficult at the current stage to claim that these images with iconic elements were the most-deleted ones, this study does exemplify a censorship deletion preference for such iconic, imagery content. Such results suggest that the adoption of image recognition technology depends on a timely human input to maintain its data set, as the inclusion of the latest elements of contested imagery, such as the iconic image of the umbrella, with high probability would have occurred *after* the censorship directive from Beijing on September 28, 2014. In other words, while the censorship mechanism on Weibo may employ an automated image recognition technology, this study suggests that the databases of such a mechanism, particularly the one targeting imagery elements, are manually and contemporaneously updated, so as to ensure the inclusion of politically sensitive multimedia content, as illustrated in the analysis. In this sense, image censorship involves not just techniques like AI and machine learning, but, more importantly, significant manual effort.

Moreover, the analysis on the removal mechanism of imagery elements confirms King et al.'s (2017, 328) theory of collective action potential, that is, censorship targets "restricting the spread of information that may lead to collective action". As shown, the removal mechanism attacks posts with imagery regarding collective action potential, regardless of whether such elements are supportive or critical of the collective action. Only those with an ambiguous attitude towards collective action have a high probability of survival. Such results demonstrate that the image removal strategy entails a deliberate manipulation to distract people from visual content about political mobilisation. These posts have greater attention-capturing capacity and a longer lifespan and thus potentially a larger influence compared to textual content (Zhao et al. 2013). Given this discussion, the censorship of multimedia and imagery posts, in particular, is to a great extent carried out by manual effort.

Conclusion and Further Studies

The censorship of the Internet in China has drawn extensive attention from academia and wider society. While previous studies have predominantly addressed censorship of online texts, this chapter investigates an under-explored dimension of content moderation: image censorship. Using a unique data set of censored and surviving multimedia posts from the Chinese social media platform Weibo during the 2014 Hong Kong UM, this study adopted visual content and framing analysis to explore and compare the censored and surviving imagery elements of the Weibo posts.

As one of the first mixed-method studies on images of conflict and censorship, this study advances empirical, theoretical and methodological discussion on the topic. Empirically, the analysis reveals that images involving recognisable elements of the UM suffered more intensive censorship. Furthermore, censorship programmes primarily target images of protests with both positive and negative attitude towards mobilisation initiatives. The empirical findings reveal that image censorship involves significant manual effort, and the image removal strategy demonstrates a deliberate manipulation by an authoritarian regime to distract people from collective action mobilisation. Theoretically, this study sheds light on content moderation criteria or mechanisms related to the visual during political contention on Chinese social media. Image-related content deletion is similar to the textual-related one recognised in King and his colleagues' study (2013): Censorship techniques strategically aim to eradicate the potentially viral process of visually affective mobilisation, be it supportive or negative attitude towards collective action mobilisation. By doing so, these findings make the first step towards extending current theories of censorship, largely established by text-based analyses, to the discussion on multimodal contention moderation.

Methodologically, this study demonstrates a mixed methodological consideration of social media analytics. The consideration reminds us to be cautious about bias and limit in the (automated) analysis of multimedia data collection, selection and analysis. More specifically, while quantitative techniques offer valuable insights about the overall picture of social media data, such techniques are also limited to produce in-depth and illustrative information in order to understand the various dimensions of the problem under analysis in a multimedia-rich reality. Instead, a combined approach allows researchers to examine a wide and refined repertoire of communicative strategies, which is a common practice online (Newhagen and Rafaeli, 1996). Such mixed analytical approaches to uncover diverse information blackout preferences and strategies towards images but also multimedia content should drive future scholarly inquiry.

This study has a number of limitations. First, it only focused on a single case, namely the UM in Hong Kong. While the analysis brings to light censorship of political events beyond the Chinese mainland, a deviant case selection (Seawright and Gerring 2008) would arguably limit the expansion of its conclusion to a general scale. I suggest that further studies with multiple cases can offer a better understanding of the different emphases of censorship and information control. Second, the coding was manual, given the exploratory nature of this study and the consideration of the complexity of multimedia content. Future research would integrate machine learning methods to differentiate genres, types or elements of multimedia modes, for instance, that help us better understand the reason behind specifically oriented censorship deletion. Third, I acknowledge that our data source is extracted from the Weiboscope project and propose that future research would integrate or compare censored content from different sources to reach a better understanding of censorship deletion in Chinese social media.

To conclude, we have conducted one of the first studies on criteria regarding multimedia censorship, with a focus on image removal. The analysis reveals that images involving prominent figures and symbols of contentious events suffered more intensive censorship. Furthermore, censorship programmes primarily target images with collective action mobilisation potential, regardless of whether the narratives of the images support or oppose mobilisation. The empirical findings hence exemplify that image censorship should involve significant manual effort, and the strategy of image removal demonstrates a deliberate manipulation by authoritarian regimes in order to distract people from politically mobilising visual content.

Funding Information

Velux Fonden, Grant/Award Number: [13143] "Images of Conflict Conflicting Images".

Acknowledgements

The author would like to thank Jingyi Zhao, Lixiong Chen and Pengnan Hu for their research assistance and the Weiboscope Open Data, which is publicly accessible by Journalism and Media Studies Centre, The University of Hong Kong (https:// jmsc.hku.hk/2016/03/weiboscope/). Moreover, the author appreciates comments and feedback from the research group "Images of Conflict, Conflicting Images" at the University of Copenhagen.

Bibliography

Aceto, G. and A. Pescapé. 2015. "Internet Censorship Detection." *Computer Networks* 83, no. 4: 381–421.

AFP and A. Beall. 2016. "Two-Thirds of Internet Users Live under Censorship as Global Online Freedom Declines for Its Sixth Straight Year." *Daily Mail*, November 14. www. dailymail.co.uk/sciencetech/article-3934602/Online-freedom-hit-pressure-social-media-apps.html

Albert, H. Y. 2016. "The Law and Politics of the Struggle for Universal Suffrage in Hong Kong, 2013–2015." *Asian Journal of Law and Society* 3, no. 1: 189–207.

Allison, A. 2000. *Permitted and Prohibited Desires*. California: University of California Press.

Bamman, D., B. O'Connor, and N. A. Smith. 2012. "Censorship and Deletion Practices in Chinese Social Media." *First Monday* 17, no. 3–5. www.uic.edu/htbin/cgiwrap/bin/ojs/index.php/fm/article/viewArticle/3943/3169

Barme, G. R. and S. Ye. 1997. "The Great Firewall of China." *Wired*, June 1. www.wired.com/1997/06/china-3/

BBC. 2014. "In Pictures: The End of Hong Kong's Mong Kok Protest Camp?" *BBC*, November 28. www.bbc.com/news/world-asia-china-30241505

Bell, P. 2011. "Content Analysis of Visual Images." In *Handbook of Visual Analysis,* edited by T. V. Leeuwen and C. Jewitt, 10–34. London: Sage.

Bhoyar, K. K and O. G. Kakde. 2010. "Skin Color Detection Model Using Neural Networks and Its Performance Evaluation." *Journal of Computer Science* 6, no. 9: 963–68.

Bil;tereyst, D., R. V. Winkel, and R. V. Winkel (eds). 2013. *Silencing Cinema*. New York: Palgrave Macmillan.

Boehler, P. 2014. "Record Censorship of China's Social Media as References to Hong Kong Protests Blocked." *South China Morning Post*, September 24. www.scmp.com/news/china-insider/article/1603869/record-censorship-chinas-social-media-references-hong-kong

Casilli, A. A. and P. Tubaro. 2012. "Social Media Censorship in Times of Political Unrest." *Bulletin of Sociological Methodology/Bulletin de Méthodologie Sociologique* 115, no. 1: 5–20.

Chan, M., X. Wu, Y. Hao, R. Xi, and T. Jin. 2012. "Microblogging, Online Expression, and Political Efficacy among Young Chinese Citizens." *Cyberpsychology, Behavior, and Social Networking* 15, no. 7: 345–349.

China Internet Watch Team. 2018. *Weibo Monthly Active Users (Mau) Grew to 431 million in Q2 2018*, August 8. www.chinainternetwatch.com/26225/weibo-q2-2018/

Coetzee, J. M. 2018. *Giving Offense*. Chicago: University of Chicago Press.

Couvares, F. G. 2006. *Movie Censorship and American Culture*. Cambridge: University of Massachusetts Press.

Deibert, R. J, J. G. Palfrey, R. Rohozinski, and J. Zittrain. 2008. *Access Denied*. Cambridge: The MIT Press

Deibert, R., J. Palfrey, R. Rohozinski, and J. Zittrain (eds). 2011. *Access Contested*. Cambridge: The MIT Press.

Deibert, R. and R. Rohozinski. 2010. "Liberation vs. Control." *Journal of Democracy* 21, no. 4: 43–57.

Dick, A. L. 2012. "Established Democracies, Internet Censorship and the Social Media Test." *Information Development* 28, no. 4: 259–260.

Dou, E. 2017. "China's Stopchat: Censors Can Now Erase Images Mid-Transmission." *The Wall Street Journal* July 18. www.wsj.com/articles/chinas-stopchat-censors-can-now-erase-images-mid-transmission-1500363950?ns=prod/accounts-wsj&ns=prod/accounts-wsj

English, D. E. 2012. "Anxiety and the Official Censorship of the Photographic Image, 1850–1900." *Yale French Studies* no. 122: 104–129.

Entman, R. M. 1993. "Framing: Toward Clarification of a Fractured Paradigm." *Journal of Communication* 43, no. 4: 51–58.

Esarey, A. and R. Kluver (eds). 2014. *The Internet in China*. Great Barrington: Berkshire Publishing Group.

Farnan, O., A. Darer, and J. Wright. 2016. "Poisoning the Well." Paper presented at the Proceedings of the 2016 ACM on Workshop on Privacy in the Electronic Society. https://doi.org/10.1145/2994620.2994636

Freedberg, D.. 1989. *The Power of Images*. Chicago: University of Chicago Press.

Friis, S. M.. 2015. "'Beyond Anything We Have Ever Seen': Beheading Videos and the Visibility of Violence in the War against Isis." *International Affairs* 91, no. 4: 725–746.

Fu, K., C. Chan, and M. Chau. 2013. "Assessing Censorship on Microblogs in China." *IEEE Internet Computing* 17, no. 3: 42–50.

Geise, S. 2017. "Visual Framing." In *The International Encyclopedia of Media Effects*, edited by P. Rössler, 1–12. New York: Wiley-Blackwell. https://doi.org/10.1002/9781118783764.wbieme0120

Gilbert, N. 2013. *Better Left Unsaid*. California: Stanford University Press.

Hansen, L. 2011. "Theorizing the Image for Security Studies." *European Journal of International Relations* 17, no. 1: 51–74.

Huang, R. and X. Sun. 2014. "Weibo Network, Information Diffusion and Implications for Collective Action in China." *Information, Communication & Society* 17, no. 1: 86–104.

Hutchinson, R. 1985. "Image of War: The Debate About Censorship." *The RUSI Journal* 130, no. 1: 37–40.

Jansen, S. C. 1988. *Censorship: The Knot That Binds Power and Knowledge*. Oxford: Oxford University Press.

Keremoğlu, E. and N. B. Weidmann. 2020. "How Dictators Control the Internet." *Comparative Political Studies* 53, no. 10–11: 1690–1703.

King, G., J. Pan, and M. E. Roberts. 2013. "How Censorship in China Allows Government Criticism but Silences Collective Expression." *American Political Science Review* 107, no. 2: 326–343.

King, G., J. Pan, and M. E. Roberts. 2014. "Reverse-Engineering Censorship in China." *Science* 345, no. 6199: 1251722.

King, G., J. Pan, and M. E. Roberts. 2017. "How the Chinese Government Fabricates Social Media Posts for Strategic Distraction, Not Engaged Argument." *American Political Science Review* 111, no. 3: 484–501.

Knockel, J., L. Ruan, M. Crete-Nishihata, and R. Deibert. 2018. *(Can't) Picture This*. August 14. https://citizenlab.ca/2018/08/cant-picture-this-an-analysis-of-image-filtering-on-wechat-moments/

Kuo, L. 2014. "Chinese Censors Are Trying to Erase Hong Kong's Pro-Democracy Movement." September 29. https://qz.com/272690/chinese-censors-are-trying-to-erase-hong-kongs-pro-democracy-movement/

Liang, B. and H. Lu. 2010. "Internet Development, Censorship, and Cyber Crimes in China." *Journal of Contemporary Criminal Justice* 26, no. 1: 103–120.

Liu, J. and J. Zhao. 2021. "More Than Plain Text." *Journal of the Association for Information Science and Technology* 72, no. 1: 18–31.

MacKinnon, R. 2008. "Flatter World and Thicker Walls?." *Public Choice* 134, no. 1–2: 31–46.

Makhortykh, M. and M. Sydorova. 2017. "Social Media and Visual Framing of the Conflict in Eastern Ukraine." *Media, War & Conflict* 10, no. 3: 359–381.

Messaris, P. and L. Abraham. 2001. "The Role of Images in Framing News Stories." In *Framing Public Life*, edited by S. D. Reese, O. H. Gandy, Jr., and A. E. Grant, 215–226. London: Routledge.

Mina, A. X. 2014. "Batman, Pandaman and the Blind Man." *Journal of Visual Culture* 13, no. 3: 359–375.

Moore, M. 2012. *China Moves to Control Sina Weibo Social Network with Real Names*. March 16. www.telegraph.co.uk/technology/news/9147767/China-moves-to-control-Sina-Weibo-social-network.html

Müller, B. 2004. "Censorship and Cultural Regulation." *Critical Studies* 22: 1–31.

Newhagen, J. E. and S. Rafaeli. 1996. "Why Communication Researchers Should Study the Internet: A Dialogue." *Journal of Communication* 46, no. 1: 4–13.

Opennet Initiative. 2005. "Internet Filtering in China in 2004–2005: A Country Study." March 20, 2019. https://opennet.net/sites/opennet.net/files/ONI_China_Country_St udy.pdf

Pan, J. 2017. "How Market Dynamics of Domestic and Foreign Social Media Firms Shape Strategies of Internet Censorship." *Problems of Post-Communism* 64, no. 3–4: 167–188.

Patterson, A. 1993. "Censorship." In *Encyclopedia of Literature and Criticism*, edited by M. Coyle, P. Garside, M. Kelsall, J. Peck, and J. Peck, 901–914. London: Routledge.

People's Daily's commentary writer. 2014. "Cherish Positive Growth: Defend Hong Kong's Prosperity and Stability." *People's Daily*, October 1. www.locpg.gov.cn/jsdt/2019-04/15/c_1210109208.htm

Qin, B., D. Strömberg, and Y. Wu. 2017. "Why Does China Allow Freer Social Media?." *Journal of Economic Perspectives* 31, no. 1: 117–140.

Ries, C. X. and R. Lienhart. 2014. "A Survey on Visual Adult Image Recognition." *Multimedia Tools and Applications* 69, no. 3: 661–688.

Roberts, M. E. 2018. *Censored: Distraction and Diversion inside Chinas Great Firewall*. Princeton: Princeton University Press.

Roberts, S. T. 2019. *Behind the Screen: Content Moderation in the Shadows of Social Media*. New Haven: Yale University Press.

Rudolph, J. 2014. "Minitrue: Delete Harmful Information on Hong Kong." *China Digital Times*, September 28. https://chinadigitaltimes.net/2014/09/minitrue-delete-harmful-information-hong-kong/

Schwalbe, C. B. and S. M. Dougherty. 2015. "Visual Coverage of the 2006 Lebanon War." *Media, War & Conflict* 8, no. 1: 141–162.

Schwalbe, C. B., B. W. Silcock, and S. Keith. 2008. "Visual Framing of the Early Weeks of the Us-Led Invasion of Iraq." *Journal of Broadcasting & Electronic Media* 52, no. 3: 448–465.

Seawright, J. and J. Gerring. 2008. "Case Selection Techniques in Case Study Research." *Political Research Quarterly* 61, no. 2: 294–308.

Sfakianakis, A., E. Athanasopoulos, and S. Ioannidis. "Censmon: A Web Censorship Monitor." *Workshop on Free and Open Communications on the Internet*. www.usenix.org/legacy/eve nts/foci11/tech/final_files/Sfakianakis.pdf

Sing Pao. 2013. "'Occupy Central' Becoming a Hot Topic among Internet Users in the Chinese Mainland." *Sing Pao*, December 25. www.singpao.com/xw/gat/201412/t2014 1225_542585.html

Staff Writer. 2018. "'Occupy' Failed Because It's Illegal." *China Daily (Hong Kong Edition)*, September 18. www.chinadaily.com.cn/hkedition/2018-09/28/content_36992468.htm

Sullivan, J. 2012. "A Tale of Two Microblogs in China." *Media, Culture & Society* 34, no. 6: 773–783.

Sullivan, J. 2014. "China's Weibo: Is Faster Different?". *New Media & Society* 16, no. 1: 24–37.

Xu, X., Z. M. Mao, and J. A. Halderman. 2011. "Internet Censorship in China." In *Passive and Active Measurement*, edited by G. F. Riley, 133–142. London: Springer.

Yu, L. L., S. Asur, and B. A. Huberman. 2015. "Trend Dynamics and Attention in Chinese Social Media." *American Behavioral Scientist* 59, no. 9: 1142–1156.

Yu, N. and Q. Xu. 2016. "Public Discourse on Genetically Modified Foods in the Mobile Sphere." In *Mobile Media, Political Participation, and Civic Activism in Asia*, edited by R. Wei, 81–102. London: Springer.

Zhao, X., F. Zhu, W. Qian, and A. Zhou. 2013. "Impact of Multimedia in Sina Weibo: Popularity and Life Span." In *Semantic Web and Web Science*, edited by J. Li, G. Qi, D. Zhao, W. Nejdl, H. Zheng, 55–65. New York: Springer-Verlag.

Zhu, T., D. Phipps, A. Pridgen, J. R. Crandall, and D. S. Wallach. 2013. "The Velocity of Censorship." *The 22nd USENIX Security Symposium*, Washington, D.C. www.usenix.org/conference/usenixsecurity13/technical-sessions/paper/zhu

7

#PRAYFORARIANA

Ritual Solidarity, Redirected Grief and Fan Commemoration on Instagram after the Manchester Arena Attack

Ally McCrow-Young

Over 20,000 fans flocked to see pop star Ariana Grande perform her sold-out show at Manchester Arena in the United Kingdom on May 22, 2017. As fans departed the show, an explosion shook the foyer of the arena, killing 22 people and injuring more than 800. The suicide bomb attack was quickly claimed by the so-called Isis,[1] and the incident became the deadliest terror attack in the UK's recent history (Dodd et al. 2017). As the city of Manchester became a site of spontaneous memorial, so too did visual social media, where users around the world united to create and share thousands of tribute images. By the following day, users had shared almost 100,000 images with the hashtag #PrayForManchester on Instagram alone. Amongst these online communities, the most prominent and consistent were Ariana Grande's fans, known as "Arianators". This case exemplifies how the ambivalence of social media culture is increasingly interwoven with contemporary conflict events. The images shared by Grande's fans point to the incongruent way in which users engage with mediatised conflicts through image creation and sharing on a platform like Instagram, where irreverent topics, branded practices and highly personalised reflections collide.

Created and prolifically shared by Arianators, images related to Grande saturated the responses on Instagram in the hours immediately following the Manchester attack. Fans shared remixed photographs of Grande, original fan art, stylised quotes and celebrity Tweet screenshots. Diverse networked fandoms find community on Instagram, bringing with them existing cross-media fan practices, but also fusing Instagram's unique "platform vernaculars" (Gibbs et al. 2014) into their engagement with the Manchester attack. Although the fusion of cultural fan practices with an affective event like a terror attack appears highly idiosyncratic, these everyday, routine and often-commercial vernaculars increasingly reflect the way in which users engage with conflict events in today's online environment.

DOI: 10.4324/9781003176923-8

This chapter examines the way intersecting community interactions with a conflict event diversify and yet standardise expressions of public mourning, shaping the way a conflict such as the Manchester attack is constituted, but also raising tensions around redirection and co-optation of grief. It explores the way in which responses to the attack are conveyed through the lens of routine fan practices, such as celebrating Grande, but in doing so, how these risk supplanting commemoration of the attack. Despite tensions around appropriative fan engagement, the images shared by Arianators account for some of the most enduring symbols of the Manchester attack to date.

The chapter begins by first laying out the conceptual framework, addressing the intersection of mediatised mourning rituals (Pantti and Sumiala 2009; Cottle 2006b) and fan participation (Duffett 2013; Jenkins 2018). Drawing these two research traditions together fills a gap in existing literature, as neither strand alone can fully shed light on the complexities of what happens when fan culture intersects with a violent conflict. Second, the chapter provides a brief background of Instagram and the context of the Manchester Arena attack. Third, the chapter presents the analysis, beginning by exploring one of the central symbols created after the attack; the black "Super Bunny" ribbon. It then examines the communal ritual solidarity between Arianators and other pop music fandoms, where fans negotiate their personal emotions after the attack. Last, the chapter discusses the repurposing of crisis hashtags, seen in the divergent images of #PrayForAriana, examining how they contribute to shaping contemporary mediatised conflicts.

Mediatised Mourning Rituals and Fan Participation

Extant understandings of mourning rituals following violent conflict events have predominantly focused on news media, as opposed to connective settings such as Instagram (e.g. Cottle 2006b; Pantti and Wieten 2005; Morse 2018). Recently, scholars have underscored the need for more research into online ritual communication, calling for increased attention to connective media and mourning rituals following public crises (Sumiala 2015; Morse 2018). This chapter, therefore, addresses the gap in existing literature by bringing together fandom and ritual perspectives in the context of a connective space – Instagram. The expanded participatory opportunities for everyday users through connective media highlight the need for an approach that acknowledges the differences between top-down and bottom-up perspectives.

Sudden and particularly violent death provokes feelings of fear and anxiety in society, disturbing systems of routine and ideas of safety, often leading to "spontaneous rituals" around these events (Haney et al. 1997). Exceptional mediatised events such as the Manchester Arena attack are closely connected to "mediatised rituals", establishing key sites where rituals are observed and enacted (Couldry et al. 2010), understood as "mediatised mourning rituals" (Pantti and Sumiala 2009). Mediatised mourning rituals are conceptualised as "a multi-layered performative practice closely connected with the workings of the media" (Sumiala

2015, 945). Contemporary literature on mediatised ritual largely acknowledges the foundational work of Emile Durkheim in *The Elementary Forms of
the Religious Life* (1912) as informing the development of ritual studies (e.g.
Pantti and Sumiala 2009; Cottle 2006b). In this work, Durkheim argues that
ceremonial rituals are central to maintaining social cohesion, where the primary
purpose of rituals is

> ... maintaining and restoring social unity through core symbols and the gen-
> eration of collective sentiments, the channelling of social conflict and per-
> suading members of a society to conform to the common values and norms.
>
> *Pantti and Sumiala 2009, 122*

Mediatised disasters such as terror attacks thus create spaces for public emotion,
such as individual and collective sense-making and consolation. Rituals following
mediatised disasters thus function on several levels to encourage self-reflection
in terms of collective identity (Cottle 2006b, 422; see also, Cottle and Nolan
2007). In this sense, notions of performativity and participation are central to
conceptualisations of mediatised ritual. For mediatised rituals, performativity is
undertaken by both media producers and consumers as part of mediatised ritual.
Stylistic conventions such as the interplay between aesthetic symbols equate to a
performance which, combined with participation, define a ritual (Rothenbuhler
1998, 111–112).

The participatory and performative aspects of mediatised ritual are similar
to the networked quality of fandom, where individual identities, as well as collective interests, are drawn together (Jenkins et al. 2013, 166). Scholarship on media
fandom is extensive and diverse, mapping fan practices and conceptualising fandom
through the evolution of multiple historic and contemporary media. At a base level,
fandom denotes individual "investment in a particular object or idea" (Seregina
and Schouten 2016, 107), such as an aspect of popular culture, often entertain-
ment culture such as films and music (Duffett 2013). Although fandom is not a
recent concept, the increased access afforded by online technologies has led to the
expansion of fandom communities (Jenkins 2012) Thus, fandom has been often
conceptualised as "an aspect of participatory culture" (Booth 2018, 3) where fans
form networks to express individual creativity (L. Bennett 2014), evaluate meanings
of popular texts (Booth 2018) and participate in civic action and education (Brough
and Shresthova 2012).

Previous research has explored the connection between fan activity and ritual
engagement through analyses of sports fandom (e.g. Cottingham 2012; Serazio
2013) and music fandom (Duffett 2015). These works highlight the role of collective effervescence and emotion in stimulating fandom solidarity, often formed
around a central "totem" or symbol (Cottingham 2012; Duffett 2013). The communal and participatory aspect of fandom research is particularly useful for analysing the myriad celebrity images related to Grande shared on Instagram after the
Manchester attack. While commemorating the attack, these users simultaneously

engage within their own communities of shared interest, such as popular music fandom. In this respect, the lens of fandom helps to illuminate contemporary connective media dynamics, showing that "mediatised disasters" (Cottle 2006a) are often shaped by everyday interests.

The Platform: Instagram

Launched in 2010, Instagram is an application for mobile photo and video sharing. In 2012, it was acquired by Facebook, remaining a separately branded app, but with increasingly extended integration with Facebook (Hill 2018). Instagram is one of the most popular platforms worldwide, topping the combined users of Snapchat, Twitter and Pinterest (Chaykowski 2016), and increasing by 100 million users each month (Etherington 2017). To date, users have shared more than 50 billion images on Instagram, averaging 4.2 billion likes per day (Aslam 2020). Instagram's global user demographics predominantly comprises young people (Kemp 2019), with more than half of the platform's users worldwide below the age of 34 (Clement 2019). In recent years, Instagram has become synonymous with popular culture, and is now one of the most influential contemporary social networking platforms as a "conduit for communication in the increasingly vast landscape of visual social media cultures" (Leaver et al. 2020, 1). It is therefore a key site through which to research a wide spectrum of social patterns from a bottom-up perspective.

Despite the popularity of Instagram and the centrality of visual social media to contemporary communicative practices, research examining the platform has so far been scarce (Leaver et al. 2020). In particular, research examining online responses to contemporary terror attacks has predominantly centred on text-based analyses, specifically Twitter (e.g. Burnap et al. 2014; Frey 2018; Smyrnaios and Ratinaud 2017). Similarly, research on coping with trauma in the aftermath of terror attacks has also focused on text practices in connective settings (e.g. Heverin and Zach 2012; Nurmi 2012; Eriksson 2016). While these works centre on contemporary case studies that are similar to this chapter, such as the terror attacks in Paris and Stockholm in recent years, they do not specifically address user-generated *visual* content (McCrow-Young 2020b). Little attention has been given to analysing how everyday individuals use image-sharing on Instagram as a way of responding to and dealing with terror attacks. This chapter thus expands research on the role of Instagram and its vernacular user cultures in the wake of mediatised disasters such as terror attacks.

The Case: Manchester Arena

On 22 May 2017, Grande's concert concluded at Manchester Arena, when a suicide bomber detonated a homemade explosive device in the foyer. As mentioned, the incident was the deadliest terror attack in the United Kingdom in over a decade (Dodd et al. 2017), the previous one being the London bombings in

2005 (Anderson 2017). The attack was part of a series of global terror attacks at the time claimed by the so-called Isis (Bennhold et al. 2017). Following the news of the Manchester Arena incident, Instagram users shared hundreds of thousands of images paying tribute to the victims of the attack, to Grande and to the city of Manchester. Grande-related images dominated the primary event hashtags #PrayForManchester and #ManchesterAttack. The images were primarily created by the Grande's large fan base, called "Arianators", who predominantly consist of teenage females (Sullivan 2017). Grande has a significant following on Instagram, with 279 million followers at the time of writing. Arianators shared images that included curated photographs of Grande's face, often overlaid with personalised text or emojis, a plethora of stylised artwork of Grande, and a customised black ribbon image superimposed with Grande's signature "Super Bunny" ears.

Methodology

The empirical scope of this chapter addresses the case of the 2017 Manchester Arena attack, analysing image post data from two broad event hashtags – #PrayForManchester and #ManchesterAttack – on the day after the incident, 23 May 2017. It draws on prior work from a broader project mapping image-sharing practices on Instagram following the Manchester attack (McCrow-Young 2020b). The chapter adopts an original method for analysing Instagram data – "connective visual mapping" (McCrow-Young 2021), which responds to the scarcity of research methods for Instagram. Existing research has primarily focused on analyses of Twitter as a site for user engagement with terror attacks, and Instagram, in particular, has been overlooked (e.g. Frey, 2018, Smyrnaios and Ratinaud, 2017, Burnap et al. 2014, Eriksson, 2016).

I, therefore, developed the platform-specific method of "connective visual mapping" to address the dynamic site of the networked image and its environment, using a number of digital tools to collate and analyse data. Connective visual mapping follows the "natural logic" of Instagram (Caliandro and Gandini 2017, 62), by acknowledging the unique vernacular practices of the platform (McCrow-Young 2020b). For example, the way common social media markers such as hashtags perform different functions on Instagram compared to platforms such as Twitter. It comprises two "mapping" processes: *macro mapping* of tag data and *micro mapping* of specific examples and profile connections within the platform interface.

For the macro-mapping process, I collated all hashtags and account tags from the metadata and by manual extraction using the platform. I then created an overview of tag practices across the dataset, to identify the average numbers of hashtags and account tags per post, and the number of unique hashtags in total. Following this, the micro-mapping process involved noting recurrent visual and textual patterns such as similar images, and flagging these examples of interest. I used two micro-mapping processes to analyse these flagged examples, firstly exploring user profiles and connections using the platform interface, and secondly conducting image searches using online tools such as reverse image search engines. The following analytical sections weave together these two mapping strands, allowing for a close examination of fandom and ritual engagement with the Manchester attack. For in-depth reflections on the ethical and technical dimensions of connective visual mapping, see (McCrow-Young 2020a, 2021).

Incongruent Images: Everyday Engagement Meets Violent Conflict

Among the images shared by users on Instagram after the Manchester attack, three central categories emerge from the confluence of fandom and ritual engagement, which I address in the following sections. Firstly, I examine the dominant image in this case – a custom black ribbon awareness ribbon, depicting a stylised version of Grande's signature "Super Bunny" ears. Secondly, I explore the remixed images demonstrating communality and ritual solidarity across networked fan communities. Thirdly, I examine the category of images that relate to #PrayForAriana, in which fans share an abundance of photographs of Grande, directing their primary feelings of grief towards her. Each category highlights the way everyday, personalised and branded vernaculars increasingly inform user engagement with a crisis event such as the Manchester attack, significantly contributing to how these events are characterised and collectively understood.

Branding the Black Ribbon?

A key image in this case was a customised black ribbon symbol on a pink background, adorned with Grande's bunny ears. It was first shared by Grande's friend and fellow celebrity Hailee Steinfeld on Twitter (Saunders 2017), and was then remixed and shared widely on Instagram by Arianators and the wider public. Grande first appeared wearing a black latex headdress with large bunny ears on the cover of her 2016 album *Dangerous Woman*. This outfit soon became one of her signature looks, with Grande referring to it as her "Super Bunny" alter ego (Martins 2016). Individuals, corporations and charities alike have adopted ribbons to demonstrate awareness of various social and political causes, and the black ribbon, in particular, has been adopted as a symbol of public mourning in response to global terror attacks, becoming "symbolic of a collective tragedy, a collective desire to mourn and to express outrage" (Moore 2010, 87). Historically, the ribbon symbol has been wrought with contradiction, stemming from the fact that

> The ribbon is … both a kitsch fashion accessory, as well as an emblem that expresses empathy; it is a symbol that represents awareness, yet requires no knowledge of a cause; it appears to signal concern for others, but in fact prioritises self-expression.
>
> *Moore 2010, 2*

These ambiguities are particularly apparent in the widespread sharing of the "Super Bunny" black ribbon in the days after the Manchester attack, which was met with polarised reactions, with some arguing that the addition of bunny ears to a mourning symbol was disrespectful and self-promotional, while others whole-heartedly supported the symbol (Simon 2017). Those opposing the use of the bunny ribbon argued that adding an iconic Grande element to an existing icon of mourning essentially functioned as branding and publicity for Grande, rather than focusing on the tragedy of the event (Robinson 2017). For example, one user on Twitter remarked, "If it's a terrorist attack, I don't feel the black ribbon with bunny ears is appropriate. It turns the tragedy into promo for Ariana ..." (@frozenghost 2017).

Mirroring the tension over branding versus public mourning through the black ribbon is the tension between the personalisation of mourning and col-lective mourning. This is evident in the various remixing practices carried out by users in this case, which personalise the black ribbon according to their own needs. Users commonly superimpose additional text with the ribbon icon, adding various backgrounds, colours and captions. While the symbol itself is repeated, users add their own meaning to it, sharing personal details often in first person diary-style and centring their post around deeply personal sentiments. For example, one user captions their remixed ribbon image stating: "Normally I wish I were [sic] in Manchester to see my idol Arian but my mom told me that I have exams, always listening to my mother ... We're so sorry for what happened in Manchester yes-terday #PrayForManchester".

These ribbon remixes demonstrate the way the personal anchors engagement with the Manchester attack, and traditional mourning symbols are drawn into individualised lifestyles and expressions, such as fandom. The additional comments further highlight the personalisation of mourning rituals in this case, which are both formed around individual emotion and anecdotes – such as referring to their mother – while also engaging with collective sentiment about the attack. Such examples illustrate the interplay between *personal* emotion and *universal* applications of the ribbon symbol. Rather than being "at odds" with each other (Moore 2010, 2), these two elements fuse, pointing to the heterogeneity of public mourning rit-uals on Instagram. As a highly spreadable (Jenkins, Ford, and Green 2013, 36) ritual symbol originating from Grande's fans, these images extend beyond fan communi-ties, evidenced by its mainstream media coverage and the popularity of the symbol on Instagram.

Ritual Solidarity and Cross-Fandom Community

A broader sense of community is also apparent in the second category of images reflecting the collective solidarity aspect of mediatised rituals *and* the common bond of networked fandoms. Fans share custom and remixed images with their existing fandom communities, helping to "discover they are not alone" (Deller

2014, 237) in the hours following the attack. Within the Arianators fandom, users often share original images they created after the attack to demonstrate support for their own community. Rather than centring the self and personal reactions to the attack in these images, users make active attempts to foster unity, reflecting the way in which networked fandoms are "bound together through their 'shared sociality' and 'shared identity'" (Jenkins et al. 2013, 166). A prominent example created by an Arianator depicts several collated profile pictures of other users in their fan community who updated their profile images of the black ribbon following the attack, surrounding the phrase "Fandom Strength".

Not only do these images visually and textually emphasise collective solidarity, but users frequently employ vernacular tag practices common to Instagram to reach wider publics. Although Instagram's tagging function is similar to that on other platforms, tagging takes on added importance on Instagram, as it serves indexical and visibility purposes for individual posts. Tags are necessary for users seeking to expand their audiences, as without tags, each new post only appears in the feed of the user's followers, limiting the post's reach. Additionally, tags allow posts to be indexed in the platform's "Explore" feed, in hashtag streams and on individual user pages, thus enabling users outside a follower network to see and engage with the posts. This pragmatic function and architecture of tags is unique to Instagram and feeds into its specific "platform vernacular" (Gibbs et al. 2014) as it requires users to adopt constant and multiple tagging practices. Therefore, tagging serves to index the user's post for multiple publics, making the offer of help visible to broader fandom communities – for example, #arianagrande – *and* the event conversations of #PrayForManchester on Instagram.

In addition to intra-fandom responses to the Manchester attack on Instagram, users also frequently make reference to the need for support *between* pop music fandoms – often referred to as "bandoms". Examples of cross-fandom images demonstrate continuous attempts at connections between networked fan communities, predominantly between fan accounts on Instagram, such as the pop music fandoms of Selena Gomez, Justin Bieber and One Direction. A widely shared image after the attack was a custom drawing depicting outstretched hands beside a list of different fandoms. The image depicts the names of 10 pop music fandoms, such as "Camilizers" – Camila Cabello's fandom and "Smilers" – Miley Cyrus' fandom, beside a hand reaching out towards Arianators. The image was shared by multiple fan accounts on Instagram on the day following the attack, such as Shawn Mendez fan accounts.

The repeated sharing of fandom unity images across multiple networked fandoms on Instagram illustrates the ritualised practice of seeking and providing emotional support in the wake of the Manchester attack, where the victims were pop music fans. These images represent a form of therapeutic communication that often emerges in the wake of public crises, in order to assist in collective healing (Sumiala and Tikka 2010, 24). Through the re-sharing and re-creating of such images, and the use of hashtag chains, users connect to diverse publics both directly and indirectly related to the attack.

Although these images of fandom solidarity reflect several positive aspects of public engagement after conflicts, they also point to the heterogeneity of such engagement, where common purposes of collective unity are not always clear-cut. These incongruities are exemplified in the many celebrity Tweet screenshots shared by users in response to the Manchester attack, for example, by pop music fandoms, such as Justin Bieber's fans, "Beliebers". In these images, other "bandoms" acknowledge the Manchester attack through the lens of their admiration for their fan object, yet make no reference to the need to support other fandom communities. Users frequently adopt large numbers of hashtags, however, these are highly tangential to the attack, serving two separate purposes of indexing their post within fandom-specific communities on the platform and expressing adoration for their fan object. For example, the hashtags adopted by one Bieber fan account lists practical details related to Bieber and his career, such as tour names – for example, #purposeworldtour – and conveys fandom phrases – for example, #bieberfamily #belieberforever.

These types of images demonstrate a focus on increasing users' personal follower base and engagement through these screenshot posts, both adding #like4like and #follow4follow. Tag practices such as these are widely used on Instagram and other follower-based social media platforms by users seeking to gain more followers through the apparent exchange of following other users in return (Abidin 2018). The addition of these often spurious, yet popular, platform practices are common in this case, illustrating the contradictions arising from the intersection of fandoms with a violent incident like the Manchester attack on Instagram. Seemingly antithetical vernaculars are thus drawn into mourning discourses surrounding the attack.

Further contradictory examples of stratified public mourning appear in the plethora of images shared by fans using #PrayForAriana. As seen above, Arianators often share images expressing collective concerns for their fandom members globally and those who were victims of the attack. However, many users share images that seek personal closure following the attack, and redirect their concern to the emotional impact of the attack on their fan object, Grande. In addition to the event hashtags #PrayForManchester and #ManchesterAttack, several fandom-centred hashtags emerged on the day immediately following the attack, the most prominent of which was #PrayForAriana. Fans frequently create images with the text #PrayForAriana superimposed onto images of Grande, as well as including variants of this sentiment in the caption, such as, #StayStrongAri, #PrayForAri and #istandwithariana. While these images still represent a form of ritual engagement, such ritualised fan activity redirects mourning sentiments towards Grande.

Fans also share a large number of images commemorating Grande alongside condolence-style text, such as images of Grande's smiling face with captions that offer reflections about her character. The images become part of fans' personal mourning for their fan object, commemorating Grande in joyful moments, and seemingly eulogising Grande's life, even though she has not passed away. In these images, there is a continued substitution of Grande as the primary victim of the attack. While demonstrating support for Grande, these images particularly highlight the plurality of interests that exist within public responses to the Manchester attack. Fandom engagement on Instagram with the Manchester attack thus embodies multiple positions, where users adopt simultaneous roles of fans and mourners through the images they share.

Expressions of solidarity and concern towards Grande's personal well-being by fans on Instagram are perhaps unsurprising given that she is their fan object, but this redirection of focus at times eclipses mourning for the victims of the attack. In these practices, there is a deliberate repurposing of event-specific hashtags by fandoms. Hashtags that have become commonly associated with online responses to terror events, such as #PrayForX and #XStrong are adapted by Arianators on Instagram, shifting the focus from solidarity towards the event to solidarity towards the fan object, Grande. "Irreverent" hashtag use (Highfield 2016) not only pertains to a contradictory application of hashtags with visual content here, but in the morphed versions of event hashtags themselves. Through such posts, fans commandeer event-specific hashtags, saturating them with Grande fandom content, but also creating new vernacular responses that modify the grief practices of #PrayForManchester.

Conclusion

In the immediate hours following the terror attack at the Manchester Arena, fans shared ritualised, emotional and personal images of their fan object, Grande – a practice they are accustomed to doing as part of their daily fandom engagement. What these images underscore is the incongruence of conflict responses in a connective space like Instagram, which are simultaneously self-promotional, personally expressive, branded and collectively engaged. This convergence of extraneous topics with post-conflict mourning reflects the ambivalence of today's online participatory spaces (Phillips and Milner 2017), where users carry out polysemic self-performances (Papacharissi 2012), weaving events like Manchester into their everyday narratives.

The fandom images in this case significantly shape the mediatised representation of the Manchester attack, where images of Grande become central to the construction of the event. The positive participatory potential of cross- and intra-fandom is evident in the communal images, such as outstretched hands, where individual responses are connected to broader networks of pre-existing fandoms on Instagram. However, routine fan practices, such as the popularity of calls to "pray for Ariana" risk trivialising such affective events, and repeated sharing of the fan object and celebration of Grande often supplant commemoration for victims. This redirection of grieving towards Grande by fans is particularly poignant given the lack of images of victims shared on Instagram following the attack (see McCrow-Young 2020b). To this day, Grande fans continue to share regular images of Grande on Instagram under the hashtag #PrayForAriana,[2] images which are disconnected from the Manchester attack by both time and content. This continued engagement by Arianators highlights the repurposing of commemorative vernacular practices on Instagram in order to fulfil fandom agendas.

Similarly, the tensions surrounding the widely shared black Super Bunny ribbon underscores the confluence of private and public perspectives, where visual displays of commemoration are both highly individual and yet connected to the broader event. The issues of branding the ribbon also point to the influence of market logics on public mourning, enhanced by an increasing personalisation of politics (Bennett and Segerberg 2013). However, notwithstanding the potential for appropriative fan practices, the images shared by Arianators after the attack represent the most persistent and permanent symbols associated with the Manchester attack. The endurance of the "Super Bunny" ribbon is evident in its continued use across social media platforms such as Instagram, for example, it was shared by users to commemorate the 12-month anniversary of the Manchester attack (Duncan 2018). Although initially created and spread by Arianators, the "Super Bunny" ribbon extends beyond networked fan communities on Instagram, evidenced by its mainstream media coverage and sustained online adoption, identifies the ribbon as a key visual representation of the Manchester attack.

Fandom imagery related to the Manchester attack has similarly maintained prominence, as images of Grande continue to dominate the top posts of both #ManchesterAttack and #PrayForManchester on Instagram to this day.[3] Arianators have maintained their engagement with these event-specific hashtags more than four years after the Manchester attack, and although users often share these images of Grande to commemorate the attack, the majority of the images are unrelated and instead focus solely on fan content. Similar divergent images can be seen across other recent terror incidents, such as the Christchurch attack, where users co-opt the public visibility of trending event hashtags to grow their follower base.

Extraneous adaptations of event-specific hashtag markers like #PrayForAriana and commemorative celebrity-centric images highlight the ambivalence of post-conflict expressions in a space such as Instagram. In this space, multiple communities of dedicated fandoms *and* mourning publics, who often have opposing standpoints, are fused together in and around a crisis such as the Manchester attack. These diverse communities become part of the public conversation of violent conflicts, constantly blending multiple, often tangential, topics as they are anchored around the everyday self. For mediatised disasters in particular, the lens of mundane, routine cultural practices means that the ordinary becomes inextricably embedded in the extraordinary. As conflict events inevitably intersect with vernacular connective cultures and practices, they will continue to embody the ambivalence of these online spaces: anchored around the self and fusing disparate topics, individuals and publics with mourning.

Notes

1 I adopt the acronym "Isis" for the "Islamic State of Iraq and Syria". The group has been referred to by several names, such as ISIL, ISIS, Islamic State or IS by news media, by

researchers and political leaders alike (Sanchez 2017). The use of various names for this group has been debated since its emergence (see, e.g. Kingsley 2014), with some suggesting the use of the Arabic acronym "Daesh" or "Daiish" (e.g. Khan 2016), in order to de-legitimise the group's claim to be a state. The adoption of the term also follows its predominant use in this case for consistency, as the group is often referred to by this acronym in news media coverage of the event.

2 #prayforariana has 50,102 posts – including current posts up until the time of writing, 1 March 2021.

3 Fandom images represented the "Top posts" as they appear in the Explore feed for the hashtags #ManchesterAttack and #PrayForManchester on Instagram as of 12 December 2020.

Bibliography

Abidin, C. 2018. *Internet Celebrity, Understanding Fame Online*. Edited by C. Abidin. Bingley: Emerald Publishing Limited.

Anderson, D. 2017. *Attacks in London and Manchester, March–June 2017*.

Aslam, S. 2020. "Instagram by the Numbers: Stats, Demographics & Fun Facts." *Omnicore* (blog), September 26. www.omnicoreagency.com/instagram-statistics/

Bennett, L. 2014. *Fan/Celebrity Interactions and Social Media: Connectivity and Engagement in Lady Gaga Fandom*.

Bennett, W. L. and A. Segerberg. 2013. *The Logic of Connective Action, Digital Media and the Personalization of Contentious Politics*. Edited by W. L. Bennett and A. Segerberg. Cambridge: Cambridge University Press.

Bennhold, K., S. Erlanger, and C. Yeginsu. 2017. "Terror Alert in Britain Is Raised to Maximum as ISIS Claims Manchester Attack." *The New York Times*. Accessed December 3, 2019. www.nytimes.com/2017/05/23/world/europe/manchester-arena-attack-ari ana-grande.html

Booth, P. 2018. *A Companion to Media Fandom and Fan Studies*. Newark: John Wiley & Sons, Incorporated.

Brough, M. M. and S. Shresthova. 2012. "Fandom Meets Activism: Rethinking Civic and Political Participation." *Transformative Works and Cultures* 10: 50 paragraphs.

Burnap, P., M. Williams, L. Sloan, O. Rana, W. Housley, A. Edwards, V. Knight, R. Procter, and A. Voss. 2014. "Tweeting the Terror: Modelling the Social Media Reaction to the Woolwich Terrorist Attack." *Social Network Analysis and Mining* 4, no. 1: 1–14. https://doi. org/10.1007/s13278-014-0206-4

Caliandro, A. and A. Gandini. 2017. *Qualitative Research in Digital Environments, a Research Toolkit*. Edited by A. Caliandro and A. Gandini. New York: Routledge.

Chaykowski, K. 2016. "Instagram, The $50 Billion Grand Slam Driving Facebook's Future: The Forbes Cover Story." *Forbes*. www.forbes.com/sites/kathleenchaykowski/ 2016/08/01/instagram-the-50-billion-grand-slam-driving-facebooks-future-the-for bes-cover-story/

Clement, J. 2019. "Distribution of Instagram Users Worldwide as of October 2019, by Age and Gender." *Statista*. Accessed January 20. www.statista.com/statistics/248769/age-distr ibution-of-worldwide-instagram-users/

Cottingham, M. D. 2012. "Interaction Ritual Theory and Sports Fans: Emotion, Symbols, and Solidarity." *Sociology of Sport Journal* 29, no. 2: 168–185. https://doi.org/10.1123/ ssj.29.2.168

Cottle, S. 2006a. *Mediatized Conflict*. Berkshire: Open University Press.

Cottle, S. 2006b. "Mediatized Rituals: Beyond Manufacturing Consent." *Media, Culture & Society* 28, no. 3: 411–432. https://doi.org/10.1177/0163443706062910

Cottle, S. and D. Nolan. 2007. "Global Humanitarianism and the Changing Aid-Media Field: 'Everyone Was Dying for Footage.'" *Journalism Studies* 8, no. 6: 862–878. https://doi.org/10.1080/14616700701556104

Couldry, N., A. Hepp, and F. Krotz. 2010. *Media Events in a Global Age.* Edited by N. Couldry, A. Hepp, and F. Krotz. London: Routledge.

Deller, R. A. 2014. "A Decade in the Life of Online Fan Communities." In *The Ashgate Research Companion to Fan Cultures*, edited by A. Widholm, L. Duits, S. Reijnders, and K. Zwaan. Farnham: Ashgate Publishing Ltd.

Dodd, V., H. Pidd, K. Rawlinson, H. Siddique, and E. MacAskill. 2017. "At Least 22 Killed, 59 Injured in Suicide Attack at Manchester Arena." *The Guardian*, May 23. Accessed January 7, 2020. www.theguardian.com/uk-news/2017/may/22/manchester-arena-police-explosion-ariana-grande-concert-england

Duffett, M. 2013. "Applying Durkheim to Elvis." *Transatlantica: Revue d'Études Américaines* 2.

Duffett, M. 2015. "Elvis' Gospel Music: Between the Secular and the Spiritual?" *Religions* 6, no. 1: 182–203. https://doi.org/10.3390/rel6010182

Duncan, A. 2018. "Fans Share Ariana Grande Symbol to Remember Manchester Attack Victims." *Metro UK*, May 22. Accessed October 27, 2019. https://metro.co.uk/2018/05/22/fans-share-ariana-grande-symbol-bunny-ears-logo-used-remember-manchester-attack-victims-7567028/

Eriksson, M. 2016. "Managing Collective Trauma on Social Media: The Role of Twitter after the 2011 Norway Attacks." *Media, Culture & Society* 38, no. 3: 365–380. https://doi.org/10.1177/0163443715608259

Etherington, D. 2017. "Instagram Now Has 800 Million Monthly and 500 Million Daily Active Users." *Tech Crunch.* Accessed February 20, 2020. https://techcrunch.com/2017/09/25/instagram-now-has-800-million-monthly-and-500-million-daily-active-users/

Frey, E. 2018. "'Do You Tweet When Your Friends Are Getting Shot?' Victims' Experience with, and Perspectives on, the Use of Social Media during a Terror Attack." *Social Media + Society* 4. https://doi.org/10.1177/2056305117750715

Frozen Ghost. 2017. If it's a terrorist attack, I don't feel the black ribbon with bunny ears is appropriate. It turns the tragedy into promo for Ariana…

Gibbs, M., J. Meese, M. Arnold, B. Nansen, and M. Carter. 2014. "#Funeral and Instagram: Death, Social Media, and Platform Vernacular." *Information, Communication & Society*: 1–14. https://doi.org/10.1080/1369118X.2014.987152

Haney, C. A., C. Leimer, and J. Lowery. 1997. "Spontaneous Memorialization: Violent Death and Emerging Mourning Ritual." *OMEGA — Journal of Death and Dying* 35, no. 2: 159–171. https://doi.org/10.2190/7U8W-540L-QWX9-1VL6

Heverin, T. and L. Zach. 2012. "Use of Microblogging for Collective Sense-Making during Violent Crises: A Study of Three Campus Shootings." *Journal of the American Society for Information Science and Technology* 63, no. 1: 34–47. https://doi.org/10.1002/asi.21685

Highfield, T. 2016. *Social Media and Everyday Politics.* Edited by T. Highfield. Oxford: Wiley.

Hill, K. 2018. "10 Reasons Why Facebook Bought Instagram." *Forbes.* Accessed January 6, 2020. www.forbes.com/sites/kashmirhill/2012/04/11/ten-reasons-why-facebook-bought-instagram/

Jenkins, H. 2018. "Fandom, Negotiation, and Participatory Culture." In *A Companion to Media Fandom and Fan Studies*, edited by P. Booth, 13–26. Newark: John Wiley & Sons, Incorporated.

Jenkins, H. 2012. *Textual Poachers: Television Fans and Participatory Culture.* 2d ed. New York: Routledge.

Jenkins, H., S. Ford, and J. B. Green. 2013. *Spreadable Media, Creating Value and Meaning in a Networked Culture.* Edited by H. Jenkins, S. Ford, and J. B. Green. New York: New York University Press.

Kemp, S. 2019. "The State of Digital in April 2019: All the Numbers You Need to Know." *We are social* (blog). January 20. https://wearesocial.com/blog/2019/04/the-state-of-digital-in-april-2019-all-the-numbers-you-need-to-know

Khan, Z. 2016. "Call It Daesh, Not ISIL (or ISIS)." *CNN.* Accessed January 7, 2020. www.cnn.com/2016/10/05/opinions/daesh-not-isil-or-islamic-state-khan/index.html

Kingsley, P. 2014. "Call Islamic State QSIS Instead, Says Globally Influential Islamic Authority." *The Guardian,* August 27. Accessed January 7, 2020. www.theguardian.com/world/2014/aug/27/islamic-state-isis-al-qaida-separatists-iraq-syria

Leaver, T., T. Highfield, and C. Abidin. 2020. *Instagram: Visual Social Media Cultures.* Cambridge: Polity.

Martins, C. 2016. "Billboard Cover: Ariana Grande on Defending Female Pop Stars and Staying Away from Drama." *Billboard.*

McCrow-Young, A. 2020a. "Approaching Instagram Data: Reflections on Accessing, Archiving and Anonymising Visual Social Media." *Communication Research and Practice*: 1–14. https://doi.org/10.1080/22041451.2020.1847820.

McCrow-Young, A. 2020b. "Incongruent Images: Connective Mourning Rituals on Instagram Following the 2017 Manchester Arena Attack." PhD dissertation, Det Humanistiske Fakultet, Københavns Universitet.

McCrow-Young, A. 2021. "Connective Visual Mapping: A Methodological Approach to Analysing Instagram Data." *Academia Letters* 6. https://doi.org/https://doi.org/10.20935/AL200

Moore, S. E. H. 2010. *Ribbon Culture, Charity, Compassion and Public Awareness.* Basingstoke: Palgrave Macmillan.

Morse, T. 2018. "The Construction of Grievable Death: Toward an Analytical Framework for the Study of Mediatized Death." *European Journal of Cultural Studies* 21, no. 2: 242–258. https://doi.org/10.1177/1367549416656858

Nurmi, J. 2012. "Making Sense of School Shootings: Comparing Local Narratives of Solidarity and Conflict in Finland." *Traumatology* 18, no. 3: 16–28. https://doi.org/10.1177/1534765611426787

Pantti, M. and J. Sumiala. 2009. "Till Death Do Us Join: Media, Mourning Rituals and the Sacred Centre of the Society." *Media, Culture & Society* 31, no. 1: 119–135. https://doi.org/10.1177/0163443708098251

Pantti, M. and J. Wieten. 2005. "Mourning Becomes the Nation: Television Coverage of the Murder of Pim Fortuyn." *Journalism Studies* 6, no. 3: 301–313. https://doi.org/10.1080/14616700500131893

Papacharissi, Z. 2012. "Without You, I'm Nothing: Performances of the Self on Twitter. (Report)." *International Journal of Communication (Online)*: 1989.

Phillips, W. and R. M. Milner. 2017. *The Ambivalent Internet: Mischief, Oddity, and Antagonism Online.* Oxford: Oxford: Polity Press.

Robinson, J. 2017. "Bunny Ears Ribbon: Is It an Appropriate Symbol for Manchester? – FLARE." *Flare,* May 25.

Rothenbuhler, E. W. 1998. *Ritual Communication, from Everyday Conversation to Mediated Ceremony.* Edited by E. W. Rothenbuhler. Thousand Oaks: Sage.

Sanchez, R. 2017. "ISIL, ISIS or the Islamic State?" *CNN,* 25 October. Accessed January 7 2020. www.cnn.com/2014/09/09/world/meast/isis-isil-islamic-state/index.html.

Saunders, E. 2017. "The Heartbreaking Symbol That Pays Tribute to Manchester Victims in Poignant Way." *Irish Mirror*, May 23. Accessed October 29, 2019. www.irishmirror.ie/showbiz/celebrity-news/heartbreaking-ariana-grande-symbol-pays-10479402

Serazio, M. 2013. "The Elementary Forms of Sports Fandom: A Durkheimian Exploration of Team Myths, Kinship, and Totemic Rituals." *Communication & Sport* 1, no. 4: 303–325. https://doi.org/10.1177/2167479512462017

Simon, R. 2017. "The Ariana Grande Black Bunny Ears Ribbon Is Stirring up Debate." *Bustle*, May 23.

Smyrnaios, N. and P. Ratinaud. 2017. "The Charlie Hebdo Attacks on Twitter: A Comparative Analysis of a Political Controversy in English and French." *Social Media + Society* 3, no. 1: 2056305117693647. https://doi.org/10.1177/2056305117693647 https://journals.sagepub.com/doi/abs/10.1177/2056305117693647

Seregina, Anastasia, and John W. Schouten. 2017. "Resolving identity ambiguity through transcending fandom." *Consumption Markets & Culture* 20, no. 2: 107–130.

Sullivan, C. 2017. "Arianators Assemble: Ariana Grande's Fans Weave a Web of Support." *The Guardian*, May 24. Accessed June 2, 2019. www.theguardian.com/music/2017/may/24/arianators-assemble-ariana-grandes-fans-weave-a-web-of-support

Sumiala, J. 2015. "Ritual Performance in Mediatized Conflict." In *The Dynamics of Mediatized Conflicts*, edited by M. F. Eskjær, S. Hjarvard, and M. Mortensen. New York: Peter Lang.

Sumiala, J. and M. Tikka. 2010. "'Web First' to Death. The Media Logic of the School Shootings in the Era of Uncertainty." *Nordicom Review* 31, no. 2: 17–30.

8

SEEING IMAGES FROM CONFLICT THROUGH COMPUTER VISION

Technology, Epistemology and Humans

Christina Neumayer and Luca Rossi

In this chapter, we argue that introducing machine learning techniques into the social and humanistic study of images of conflict needs to acknowledge the specific way in which computer vision *sees* the world and how computer vision is constructed. Computer vision (following a common definition by IBM 2021) is a form of artificial intelligence (AI) which is commonly understood as smart machines performing tasks that otherwise require human intelligence. If we use the ability of computers to think as a metaphor for AI, computer vision would suggest the ability to *see*. However, if modern AI defines intelligence as the ability of detecting or identifying patterns in data and operationalise this ability as something that needs to be trained, similarly modern application of computer vision requires computers to be trained to *see*. Reflecting on a process of training a computer vision system to *see* images of conflict and drawing from insights in the humanities and social sciences, we suggest a conceptual framework for tracing how computer vision learns to *see*.

As this edited volume demonstrates, scholarship in the humanities and social sciences has developed a multiplicity of conceptual and empirical ways to interpret, analyse and theorise digital images from conflict at their intersections with politics, society and culture. There are robust concepts (such as representation, genre, spectacle, meaning, semiosis, to name a few) at hand that help us to understand images from conflict. While studies focused on how such images can represent and even escalate and deescalate conflicts such as protests, terrorism and war and try to understand the complexity of images of conflicts (Blaagaard et al. 2017), it is increasingly difficult to methodologically grabble with the increasing number of images. To surpass the limits of manual analysis in the study of images from conflicts, a luring solution is the employment of computational methods. Yet, this assumes that the techniques developed within the field of computer vision can

DOI: 10.4324/9781003176923-9

simply be applied as tools that allow us to see, with higher speed or precision, the large quantity of images from conflict through the eyes of a humanities or social science scholar. Yet, can computer vision address the type of questions we ask in the study of images from conflict? How can we understand the epistemological consequences computer vision might have on studying images from conflict? And does the descriptive nature of computer vision allow us to understand concepts such as violence, iconicity or visibility in an image?

To fruitfully combine the theoretical concepts from the study of images from conflict with the potential of computer vision, we need to start by having a proper understanding of processes and underlying assumptions of what it means for computer vision "to *see* something". We develop this understanding based on our recent work that required training of a neural network to *see* and measure violence in Twitter images from the protests during the G20 in Hamburg, Germany, in 2017 (Rossi et al. 2022), and we draw on examples from the Black Lives Matter movement and the Hong Kong protests. Our conceptual understanding operates within three dimensions:

- *Technology* and problems of current computer vision solutions (Al-Faris et al. 2020) when working with a socio-culturally complex phenomenon such as the visual representation of conflict.
- *Epistemology* at intersection of humanistic and sociological inquiry, and computer vision (Goldenfein 2019).
- *Humans* both as subject of the computer vision as well as often invisible actors involved in the training of a computer vision system (Altenried 2020).

In the following, we trace the process of a computer vision system learning to *see* images from conflict along these three dimensions.

Technology: From Computer Vision to Violence in Images from Protests

In computer science, computer vision is part of the broader field of AI, and it is commonly understood as the effort to train computers to process visual data so that they can perform a specific task (e.g. recognising a face, identifying an object, counting how many people are crossing an intersection). Within this perspective, computer vision is an effort of machine learning. To train a computer vision system, it needs a set of (visual) training data that will be used to detect statistical patterns so that the specific task could be performed on new (never seen before) data. Computer vision systems designed for facial recognition, for example, are trained on large datasets composed by distinct images of faces. To build a system that can recognise different objects (e.g. differentiate between apples and pears), we need to collect and add labels to images of such objects and train a neural network on those labelled images (see Crawford and Paglen 2019). The computer vision system then statistically analyses the images and develops a model to differentiate between the two "classes". Once the process is done, the system is ready to identify these objects and entities in images, it has not seen before.

In the field of computer vision, there are two sub-areas that are of great interest for their potential applications within the study of violence in images of political protests: *object recognition* and *activity recognition*. Although a detailed analysis of the current state of the art of computer vision is outside of the scope of this chapter, introducing these two areas of research allows us to better understand the underlying assumptions of such methods and their technological limitations. *Object recognition* is concerned with the problem of recognising objects from image data and to understand their position within a 3D world (Cao 2011). A classical problem of object recognition would be to start from a digital image, process it and produce an output that could read: "In this picture there is a cat on a table". Here the computer system detects objects (the cat and the table) and a spatial relation (the cat is on the table). *Activity recognition* (Mo et al. 2016) is concerned with the analysis of video or image data to identify the activities that a person (or an entity) is doing. A classical problem would be to start from the video input of a surveillance system and produce an output that could read: "A person is entering the building" or "two persons are fighting on the street". Several variations of these general directions are possible: these tasks can be combined and integrated with other tasks such as facial recognition to produce outputs that could read like "a person in entering the building, the person is holding a gun and has an angry face, there is a high chance that the person is […]".

An illustrative example of these approaches and images from protests: We used the IBM's public Watson computer vision system (www.ibm.com/dk-en/cloud/watson-visual-recognitionan) to process an image widely shared by the Black Lives Matter movement showing video footage of former police officer Derek Chauvin pressing his knee to George Floyd's neck. The system describes the image with a series of labels including "ultramarine colour" (0.98), "dog" (0.72), "domestic animal" (0.72), "animal" (0.72), "police dog" (0.72), "person" (0.67), "sport" (0.60), "detective" (0.56) and "trooper" (0.50). Next to the labels, we find a score that tells us how likely it is for these labels to be in the picture. The system does not actually see the image (as humans would do) with the complexity of the situation and the social and racial tension it entails. It converts the image into a set of probably detected objects (dog, domestic animal, person), activities (sport) or visual patterns (ultramarine blue) with various degree of success. The goal of this example is mainly to show how a complex image is translated into a set of visual entities. Nevertheless, it is impossible to notice in the labels produced by the system – and especially in the inability of recognising a black person – signs of the systemic racist bias that affects application of machine-learning methods on visual data (for a critical discussion see e.g. Crawford and Paglen 2019; Raji et al. 2020; Zou and Schiebinger 2018).

Applying the same computer vision technology on a picture taken during the 2019 Hong Kong pro-democracy protests, the system returns a similar set of labels: "riot" (0.98), "person" (0.95), "black colour" (0.92), "gray colour" (0.74).

The label "riot" (an activity) is included in contrast to the absence of any label suggesting an "arrest" in the first case. While one may argue that this renders the labels for the second image more accurate, in both cases the output of the system *describes* the scene starting from a set of entities (colours, actors, objects) and inferring some activities, but it does not include any perception of violence or the social relationship between the actors in the pictures. In contrast, looking at the same image through human eyes would enable us to question if this is indeed a riot or the police using tear gas against protesters. This relational perspective and the nuances, politics and power in the image cannot be *seen* by computer vision beyond a mere description of the objects in the image.

Building on this baseline of how computer vision operates, we will now try to add additional insights drawn from our experience working with the Twitter images from the G20 protests in Hamburg in 2017 (Rossi et al. 2021). In this context, we trained a neural network with the aim of measuring the level of violence in the images that had been shared online during the protest event. As described above, computer vision systems need to be trained with a large amount of pre-labelled data. In our case, this was the data collected by Won et al. (2017) composed of 11,659 images of protest events in urban setting. Since our goal was to label many images with a score that would represent the level of violence in an image, we randomly sampled 58,295 pairs of images and we assigned those pairs of images to human codes who were asked to identify the most violent image of the pair they were shown (based on a method by Bradley and Terry, 1952). At the end of this process, we statistically transformed the judgement of the human coders into violence scores attached to every single image in our sample. This defined the training data that we used to analyse the Twitter images produced during the G20 protests in Hamburg. The system performed remarkably well being able to assign violence scores to the Twitter images from protest that (when manually validated) seemed perfectly reasonable. To give an example: The image of a protester marching would be scored less violent than a picture representing a confrontation with the police, and the latter would be scored as less violence than a picture where the violence degenerated in burning barricades.

Despite the good results achieved by the system, there are two aspects that are relevant to further explore for the goals of this chapter: First, to push computer vision outside of the descriptive function of the available out-of-the box systems, we had to train an ad-hoc neural network and rely on considerable technical skills and pre-existing research and resources (e.g. the images we used to train the system). This long process is far from the idea of computer vision as an off-the-shelf service which commercial products suggest. While a computer vision system may be used as a service if the goal is to count how many cats are present in a large number of images, it is important to acknowledge that questions we normally ask in the social sciences and humanities and especially in conflict contexts are more complex. Second, it is important to understand that even the system that we have trained should not be considered a tool for violence measurement in a general sense. The system was trained with labelled data from the specific context of urban protest, and it can therefore not be employed to rank violence in images from other conflicts (such as images from a war zone). The computer vision system does not see violence as a relational situation that involves humans, but it has learned to statistically associate specific visual patterns frequently occurring in urban conflicts (e.g. fire) with higher or lower scores. The system generalised from the idea of violence given by human coders who chose the more violent picture of a pair of images during the training phase. A different set of coders (e.g. from a different geographical area) or a different set of training data (such as images form war zones rather than urban protest) would have produced a different way of ranking violence.

Epistemology: Computers Seeing Images from Conflict

While we can train systems to detect violence in a specific context, computer vision cannot tease out nuances that emerge at the relationship between images and meanings. Social scientists have a long tradition of acknowledging, tracing and studying such nuances (Crawford 2021; Mattoni and Pavan 2018), but the complexities of visibility, visuality, contradictions, power and politics cannot be translated into computer vision and as Crawford and Paglen (2019) conclude, they never will. The meaning we derive from images from conflict may change over time and across cultural contexts, and images get interpreted and reinterpreted. In other words, there is no objective truth in classifying an image by computer vision, because the AI does not see with the same politics, prejudices and ideology as humans.

In the previous section we argued that the promise of computer vision as tool or a service that will help us tackling the large quantity of visual material does not hold if we ask complex questions that aim at interpreting complicated situations such as conflict. We must acknowledge how a metaphor equating the computational processing of visual data to human vision is misleading. Computer vision represents "a parallel universe composed of activations, key points, eigenfaces, feature transforms, classifiers, training sets, and the like" (Paglen 2016, not paginated). Using the metaphor of *seeing* for computer vision and conveying it with more objectivity and neutrality (due to the measurability and countability of these processes) than a human's way of seeing, can reinforce power and racial bias. Images from conflicts do not simply represent entities and objects, but they are part of struggles over visibility, power relations, aesthetics and visualities (Blaagaard et al. 2017, for an overview). The promise of objectivity renders the way computer vision sorts, classifies and regulates society (often in problematic ways) invisible, although the machine's way of *seeing* often includes race and class interests too (Paglen 2016, not paginated). Paglen (2016) encourages us to understand the "invisible world of images" – not simply as an alternative to visuality but as an "exercise of power, one ideally suited to molecular police and market operations".

How can we understand the epistemological consequences computer vision might have on studying images from conflict? Goldenfein (2019) argues that the answer to that is certainly not that we all need to learn how to code and how to train algorithmic systems. As we have shown in the previous section, computer vision (even if adequate for the task it is trained for) "operates within the dynamics of representation and knowledge, and still interacts with human visuality" (Goldenfein 2019, 111). We therefore need to understand computer vision as a way of *seeing* that is different from how humans see. Computer vision as a part of data science transforms data into statistical models with the aim of classification and detection. This process exists in connection with humans and society thus inherits bias, but it also obfuscates those behind several technical and statistical layers. In other words, it is an exercise of visual data processing and a subfield of machine learning "generating knowledge by applying data science to images in a way that transforms measurements of the world in the form of pixel vectors into classifications" (Goldenfein 2019, 110). While a computer vision system may output a description (based on labels) of the objects in an image (or video) or of a process (or what is happening), it does not interpret meaning of what it *sees*. The descriptive nature of the output of computer vision processing applied to our examples leads us to fundamental questions: Is the computational analysis of visual content able to address the type of analysis that is usually performed in the study of images from conflict? Can a description of images help us to eventually understand violent action frames, iconicity or symbols in an image?

Let us return to our work with violence in images from protests: Even before engaging with the more complex narrative that is usually built around a violent confrontation by antagonistic actors (Neumayer and Rossi 2018), the reading of the visual representation of the inherent level of violence of a single image depends on human interpretation. Violence can appear in various forms, some of which perhaps easier to identify and label than others. Conceptual understandings of violence differentiate between explicit violence, the direct execution of physical violence; latent violence, not directly executed but latent expressions of authority and/or destruction (Fishman and Marvin 2006). Differentiating between these forms of violence and identifying them in an image depends on a specific understanding of violence which depends on the social, cultural and political context of the image but also the person interpreting it. This understanding is based on a human assessment of what may turn a conflictual situation into a violent act (Kivivuori 2014) rather than entities in the image that can in their combination be classified as "violent". Such complexities are what we usually pay attention to, when we study violence in images from protest within the context of visual media, culture and politics. And while qualitative and manual content analysis methods have evolved over the years, it is uncertain if computational methods ever will accommodate the complexity of these questions if not through ad-hoc approaches that train computer vision systems for each one of these questions within a clearly defined visual and cultural context.

Such a socially and culturally complex understanding of the visual in conflict cannot be achieved by the computational empiricism that computer vision proposes – a descriptive, quantifiable approach to classify visual content. Moving from a series of detected elements (or actions) to a more comprehensive analysis of the images of conflict is far from simple, but rather than simply applying tools, we need to acknowledge that computer vision never operates on all the data an image provides but selections of it which produces invisibilities as well as overrepresentation of other aspects (Neumayer et al. 2021). This is particularly problematic when using off-the-shelf computer vision systems, where the training process is opaque, and we cannot trace how the system learned to *see* and in what context. With such developments the in-depth visual analysis of images from conflict (as all the chapters in this volume do) becomes ever more important, but we also need to start paying attention to the role computer vision and the new visualities it introduces – in the images themselves as well as when we apply computer vision in our analysis.

Humans: The People in Images from Conflict and in Computer Vision

Considering the complexity of the questions that this edited volume asks about images from conflict and more specifically the questions asked in the literature about violence in such images from protests (Neumayer et al. 2016; Neumayer and Rossi 2018), we need to pay attention to the humans in and behind such images. When we think about computer vision and its use in the field of images from conflict, we often think about the experts in data science and machine learning as humans involved into the process. Yet, there are other humans that play an essential role but are often overlooked: (a) humans depicted in the images processed by computer vision as well as in the training data; and (b) the invisible labour of humans involved into producing the training data.

To shed some light on these invisible humans, let us return to our research on violence in images from protests. For computer vision, it may be possible to imagine a system being able to identify a finite set of violent actions recognisable as entities in an image from urban protest (such as fire, batons, rubber bullets, presence of blood, etc.). Yet, it is far more challenging to train a system that could consistently put those "actions" into a ranked relationship of the level of violence. An example: a bleeding protester may be interpreted as more violent than an image depicting a protester who has been beaten up (but is not bleeding). Human perception of what appears violent is likely affected by socio-cultural background as well as the individual elements and the humans in the image (e.g. their age, gender, position, number of people, their interaction). To translate this into entity recognition: How much blood must be present in an image for a computer vision system to classify violent images containing blood more violent than pictures that do not show blood? A human coder may carefully weigh all the elements in the image but also recognise the various actors and come to a decision based on the respective socio-cultural context. We have robust theories and concepts for seeing images from protests and interpreting them in terms of their visibility (Neumayer and Rossi, 2018), visualities (Mirzoeff 2017) or indeed the role violence plays in such images (Juris 2005) and their representation in digital media (Poell and van Dijck, 2015), but computer vision does not see violence in the same way.

If computer vision cannot put the images into a broader socio-cultural or the-oretical context, questions concerning the humans in the images become highly problematic if answered by computational analysis: Who is the perpetrator? Who are the actors in the image? How are they framed? What is their gender? Are they police or protesters and who does what? To follow up on one of these examples, there are certainly challenges in training a computer vision system to identify the perpetrator of violence in an image, and this is not a problem of facial recognition (which is likely one of the most advanced uses of computer vision). Facial recogni-tion, as a problem of computer vision, can be seen as a more complex task of object recognition where the number of objects to recognise is extremely large, one indi-vidual being one "object". If we are to identify the perpetrator of violence in an image based on such analysis, such a system would be highly problematic to use – not only because it was trained for something else but also because this question entails ethical consequences. The problems of the technological development and the ethical reflection about its applications do not deal with the ability of computer vision to recognise faces but with its accuracy (especially in specific conditions such as low light), the use of uncertain results and the acquisition of the training data. This contrasts with the promises of precision and the veneer of objectivity and neu-trality computer vision is endowed with (Crawford 2021) and it becomes increas-ingly problematic when conducting analysis about humans in images from conflict.

The second group of humans often rendered invisible are the humans involved into the process of training the system. With the idea that computer vision sees independently from humans, we also tend to reduce the visibility of human labour involved into the process. In developing our computer vision system (Rossi et al. 2021), there are humans involved into training the system in various ways. This includes experts with computational competences as well as statistical model-ling, but there are also aspects concerning expertise in the specific field of the visual representation of conflict. All the decisions taken along the way in training the computer vision system and in interpreting the results require both the tech-nical and statistical expertise, and the expertise in understanding what is at stake when studying images from conflict. Recently the racial, social and gender bias in machine learning due to an overrepresentation of white men in the field of computer science developing such systems gained attention (Noble 2018; Eubanks 2018). While measures exist to understand the accuracy of a computer vision system, estimating its racial, cultural and social bias is far more difficult and lacks commonly accepted strategies. Although research is concerned with the consequences of algo-rithmic systems for humans (often referred to as the humans-in-the-loop) and the ethical concerns (Rahwan 2018), the humans behind training such systems often remain invisible.

Let us consider our work with training a computer vision system: Our work involved both, experts from the humanities and social sciences as well as computer science, but we have not yet considered the (often invisible) labour of the coders involved into labelling the data to train the system. To recruit the human coders that performed the pairwise comparison of the protest images we needed to build our training data, we employed Amazon Mechanical Turk (AMT) which has become common practice for machine learning research (Bhown et al. 2019; Hong et al. 2019) and for social science experiments that benefit from large numbers of coders (Shank, 2016). AMT and similar services have recently come under intense scrutiny. From a methodological perspective (Woike 2019) the criticism is concerned with the lack of quality of data resulting from the possibility that quotas of coded data are reached by randomly clicking through the given options. Responding to this criticism, methods were developed that allow us to detect anomalies in the behaviours of the coders, and each code can be manually inspected or excluded if the research deems it necessary. Yet, we do work with human coders, and we design a system based on which they will perform the coding. With humans involved in all stages of training the system, human prejudice, bias and ideas will inevitably be translated into the training data and into the computer vision system. To produce an estimate of the level of violence compatible with the context where the G20 images were generated (i.e. protest in Hamburg, Germany), we only employed European AMT workers. While this may have made the resulting system more accurate in the specific context of detecting violence in urban protests in the Europe, it would not be accurate in any other context. Protests may look differently in other places around the world, and there are differences in the perception of violence, which was the central concept in this research. This means that despite all the human labour that went into the process of training our computer vision system, it is not applicable beyond the specific context of our study.

Moreover, the human coders involved in such processes are not usually part of the discussion of how people are affected by algorithmic systems. From an ethical perspective (Williamson 2016), the low average wages of AMT workers have been criticised, the power imbalance that reinforces them as well as the effects that specific tasks can have on the psychological and physical well-being of the workers (Bohannon 2016). Yet, it is so far the only way to afford labelling of such large datasets. To adhere to our own standards in using AMT, we offered a salary aligned with the European cost of labour and ensured that their work was speedily approved and paid. The images in the training data, while representing urban protests, did not contain excessively disturbing content. We were in contact with the workers during and after they coded the data, and they gave us feedback on how they experienced the pairwise comparison of the images. However, from our interaction with the coders, we know that this is the exception and that their working conditions are often underprioritised, and their work underpaid.

Despite all our measures taken, uncertainties remain regarding the (often) invisible labour involved into the process. Are the AMT workers representative of a potential audience for Twitter images from the G20 protests? Would the results look different if other coders worked with the training data (despite validation of the system)? And, while we did ensure an ethical employment of AMT, do we still support a system that is based on exploitative working conditions for the purpose of advancing development of computer vision and AI? And how do we acknowledge our own bias built into the research design and the training of the computer vision system? These questions become even more pertinent for the study of images from conflict which are politically, socially and culturally sensitive. That is, what can we do to avoid the trap of simply applying tools and buying into the technical positivism, computational epistemology and the veneer of objectivity and neutrality machine learning often promises? Despite all these critical questions, we need to understand such methods and their underlying processes too, when computer vision itself plays an important role in images from conflict as an assemblage of people, practices, cameras, mobile devices, and indeed software, algorithms and machine learning processes.

Conclusion

This chapter does not conclude with a definite answer or manual of how we can employ computer vision in the study of images from conflict. Instead, we suggest a conceptual framework that allows us to unpack how computer vision learns to *see*. To understand the output of computer vision, we need to trace this process within the dimensions of technology, epistemology and humans. This is particularly pertinent in the study of images from conflict due to the complexity of representation, visibility, visuality, power and confrontation. As scholars in the humanities and social sciences, we have learned to unfold such complexities, and we need to mobilise this understanding to work alongside computer scientists when applying such methods in this field. Our conceptual understanding of the process urges us to combine knowledge about how computer vision learns to label images through scene detection or entity recognition with the complexity and cultural specificity of a socio-culturally complex concept such as violence. This process requires a variety of expertise that we need to learn to combine if we are to tackle large quantities of data in the study of images from conflict without buying into computer vision's false promise of objectivity, precision and neutrality. Taking challenges and limitations to computer vision into account might allow us to move towards a more reflective approach, which does enable us to analyse large quantities of visual content while at the same time allowing us to unfold the underlying complexities.

Developing methods that allow for a reflective use of computer vision might become a relevant endeavour for this field with AI playing an increasingly important role for the representation of conflict in digital images. Tracing the technology, epistemology and people in the process of training a computer vision system reminds us, that it ultimately reflects and serves beliefs and perspectives of people (Jakobsson et al. 2021). It may allow us to challenge assumptions of precision, and accuracy to move towards a more substantial understanding of the role such systems play in the visual representation of conflict (Suchman 2020) and ultimately, to capture its role in mediated conflict (e.g. Cottle 2006). Today, images from conflicts are processed through computer vision, produce their own images of political conflict, at the intersections of technology, epistemology and humans. If we are to understand such algorithmic actors in the field of images from conflict, moving away from understanding computer vision as a tool in our own work might be a good start.

Tracing epistemologies, technologies and humans may allow us to mobilise, build on and enhance humanistic and social inquiry into the study of images from conflict. Yet, it also reminds us to avoid oversimplification and classifications in favour of quantification and the promise of objectivity, but instead, to produce meaning by unfolding the complexity of computer vision's ways of *seeing* images from conflict.

Bibliography

Al-Faris, M., J. Chiverton, D. Ndzi, and A. I. Ahmed. 2020. "A review on computer vision-based methods for human action recognition." *Journal of Imaging* 6, no. 6: 46.

Altenried, M. 2020. "The platform as factory: Crowdwork and the hidden labour behind artificial intelligence." *Capital & Class* 44, no. 2: 145–158.

Bhown, A., S. Mukherjee, S. Yang, S. Chandak, I. Fischer-Hwang, K. Tatwawadi, and T. Weissman. 2019. "Humans are still the best lossy image compressors." In *2019 Data Compression Conference* (DCC) March, 558–558.

Blaagaard, B., M. Mortensen, and C. Neumayer. 2017. "Digital images and globalized conflict." *Media, Culture & Society* 39, no. 8: 1111–1121.

Bohannon, J. 2016. "Mechanical Turk upends social sciences." *Science* 352, no. 6291: 1263–1264.

Bradley, R. A. and M. E. Terry. 1952. "Rank analysis of incomplete block designs: I. The method of paired comparisons." *Biometrika* 39, no. 3/4: 324.

Cao, T. P. (ed.). 2011. *Object recognition*. London: IntechOpen.

Cottle, S. 2006. *Mediatized conflict: Developments in media and conflict studies*. London: McGraw-Hill Education.

Crawford, K. (2021). *The Atlas of AI*. New Haven: Yale University Press.

Crawford, K. and T. Paglen. (2019). Excavating AI: The politics of training sets for machine learning. Available at: https://excavating.ai

Eubanks, V. 2018. *Automating inequality: How high-tech tools profile, police, and punish the poor*. New York: St. Martin's Press.

Fishman, J. M. and C. Marvin. 2006. "Portrayals of violence and group difference in newspaper photographs: nationalism and media." *Journal of Communication* 53, no. 1: 32–44.

Goldenfein, J. 2019. "The profiling potential of computer vision and the challenge of computational empiricism." In *Proceedings of the Conference on Fairness, Accountability, and Transparency*, 110–119. Atlanta: Association for Computing Machinery.

Hong, J., K. Lee, J. Xu, and H. Kacorri. 2019. "Exploring machine teaching for object recognition with the crowd." In *Extended Abstracts of the 2019 CHI Conference on Human Factors in Computing Systems* 1–6.

IBM. 2021. What is computer vision? Available at: www.ibm.com/topics/computer-vision

Jakobsson, P., A. Kaun, and F. Stiernstedt. 2021. "Machine intelligences: An introduction." *Culture Machine* 20: 1–9. Available at https://culturemachine.net/vol-20-machineintelligences/

Juris, J. S. 2005. "Violence performed and imagined: Militant action, the Black Bloc and the mass media in Genoa." *Critique of Anthropology* 25, no. 4: 413–432.

Kivivuori, J. 2014. "Understanding trends in personal violence: Does cultural sensitivity matter?" *Crime and Justice* 43, no. 1: 289–340.

Mattoni, A. and E. Pavan. 2018. "Politics, participation and big data. Introductory reflections on the ontological, epistemological, and methodological aspects of a complex relationship." *Partecipazione e Conflitto* 11, no. 2: 313–331.

Mirzoeff, N. 2017. *The appearance of Black Lives matter*. Miami: NAME publications. Available at: https://namepublications.org/item/2017/the-appearance-of-black-lives-matter/

Mo, L., F. Li, Y. Zhu, and A. Huang. 2016. "Human physical activity recognition based on computer vision with deep learning model." In *2016 IEEE International Instrumentation and Measurement Technology Conference Proceedings* 1–6.

Neumayer, C. and L. Rossi. 2018. "Images of protest in social media: Struggle over visibility and visual narratives." *New Media & Society* 20, no. 11: 4293–4310.

Neumayer, C., L. Rossi, and B. Karlsson. 2016. "Contested hashtags: Blockupy Frankfurt in social media." *International Journal of Communication* 10, no. 22: 5558–5579.

Neumayer, C., L. Rossi, and D. M. Struthers. 2021. "Invisible data: A framework for understanding visibility processes in social media data." *Social Media+ Society* 7, no. 1. doi: 10.1177/2056305120984472

Noble, S. U. 2018. *Algorithms of oppression.* New York: New York University Press.

Paglen, T. 2016. "Invisible images (your pictures are looking at you)." *The New Inquiry,* December 8. Available at: https://thenewinquiry.com/invisible-images-your-pictures-are-looking-at-you/

Poell, T. and J. van Dijck. 2015. "Social media and activist communication." In *The Routledge companion to alternative and community media,* edited by C. Atton, 527–538. London: Routledge.

Raji, I. D., T. Gebru, M. Mitchell, J. Buolamwini, J. Lee, and E. Denton. 2020. "Saving face: Investigating the ethical concerns of facial recognition auditing." In *Proceedings of the AAAI/ACM Conference on AI, Ethics, and Society,* 145–151.

Rahwan, I. 2018. "Society-in-the-loop: Programming the algorithmic social contract." *Ethics and Information Technology* 20, no. 1: 5–14.

Rossi, L., C. Neumayer, J. Henrichsen, and L. Beck. 2022. "Measuring violence: A computational analysis of violence and propagation of image tweets from political protest." *Social Science Computer Review,* doi: 10.1177/08944393211055429

Shank, D. B. 2016. "Using crowdsourcing websites for sociological research: The case of Amazon Mechanical Turk." *The American Sociologist* 47, no. 1: 47–55.

Suchman, L. 2020. "Algorithmic warfare and the reinvention of accuracy." *Critical Studies on Security* 8, no. 2: 175–187.

Williamson, V. 2016. "On the ethics of crowdsourced research." *PS: Political Science & Politics* 49, no. 1: 77–81.

Woike, J. K. 2019. "Upon repeated reflection: Consequences of frequent exposure to the Cognitive Reflection Test for Mechanical Turk participants." *Frontiers in Psychology* 10: 2646.

Won, D., Z. C. Steinert-Threlkeld, and J. Joo. 2017. "Protest activity detection and perceived violence estimation from social media images." In *Proceedings of the 25th ACM International Conference on Multimedia,* 786–794.

Zou, J. and L. Schiebinger. 2018. "AI can be sexist and racist—it's time to make it fair." *Nature* 559: 324–326.

INDEX

Taylor & Francis Group
an **informa** business

Taylor & Francis eBooks

www.taylorfrancis.com

A single destination for eBooks from Taylor & Francis
with increased functionality and an improved user
experience to meet the needs of our customers.

90,000+ eBooks of award-winning academic content in
Humanities, Social Science, Science, Technology, Engineering,
and Medical written by a global network of editors and authors.

TAYLOR & FRANCIS EBOOKS OFFERS:

A streamlined
experience for
our library
customers

A single point
of discovery
for all of our
eBook content

Improved
search and
discovery of
content at both
book and
chapter level

REQUEST A FREE TRIAL
support@taylorfrancis.com

Routledge
Taylor & Francis Group

CRC Press
Taylor & Francis Group

For Product Safety Concerns and Information please contact our EU
representative GPSR@taylorandfrancis.com
Taylor & Francis Verlag GmbH, Kaufingerstraße 24, 80331 München, Germany

www.ingramcontent.com/pod-product-compliance
Lightning Source LLC
Chambersburg PA
CBHW070347270326
41926CB00017B/4021